The Light Where Shadows End

The Light Where Shadows End

A War Story Series

rg cantalupo

Published by Tablo

Published in 2019 by Tablo Publishing.

To Mariela,

With love, thanks, and gratitude
through the long years.

Table of Contents

"A masterpiece of war, suffering, and redemption."
H. H. Gregory

Acknowledgement

Grateful Acknowledgements to Donald Anderson and "War, Literature, and the Arts" where much of this book was first published.

Additional acknowledgements to "The Veteran", published by VVAW, where many excerpts were first published or reprinted.

About the Author

rg cantalupo is a poet, playwright, filmmaker, novelist, and director. His work has been published widely in literary journals in the United States, England, and Australia.

His books include The Light Where Shadows End, Kill Today, So Tomorrow Will Not Come, You Don't Know Me, Involving Residence,No Thanks, Walking Water On Earth, The Art of Naming, Private Entries, and The Endurance: Journey To Worlds End.

He served with the *25th* Infantry Division as an RTO (radio operator), for an infantry company from 1968-69 and received three purple hearts and a Bronze Star with a Combat V for Valor Under Fire.

His books can be purchased through New World Publishers (newworldpublishers.com), Amazon, or through the author at *info@rgcantalupo.com*.

What readers and critics have said about *The Light Where Shadows End:*

"Vivid, strong memories -- eloquently reported -- make this book a masterpiece of war, suffering, and redemption."
H. H. Gregory

"...the most engaging book on the subject I have ever read."
Lawrence Drake

"...a searing story of war, survival and reconciliation told by a true war hero."

C. Canton

"...as close to being in battle as any written account can be.

David Hernandez

"A page-turner that won't let you put it down!"

Jason Calhoun

"A must read!"

D. Anderson

Author's Note

For almost fifty years, ghosts haunted me in night's dead land.

They lived inside my blood, rose out of my heart's graveyard, and reached up from the earth to clutch my throat in terror dreams.

Therapy couldn't save me.

Nor drugs. Nor alcohol.

Nor living on the edge of darkness.

Nor tight-roping on the thread of death.

I was a war criminal.

I fired white phosphorous mortars and called in napalm bombs on civilians using weapons banned by the Geneva Convention.

I was a war hero.

I saved four men's lives by sacrificing my own.

I was awarded a Bronze Star with a Combat V for courage under fire and three purple hearts.

And somewhere between these two irreconcilable battles was the wreckage of my life—drugs, divorces, deadly despairs.

For twenty years, I wrote and rewrote my story, never finding a beginning or an end.

And, over the years, the ghosts multiplied, becoming a company of bad spirits asking me to join them in their graves.

In May, 2015, to survive my looming suicide, I returned to the field where I died.

I do not know what I expected to find there.

Surely not my bones, nor the bones of so many friends and

enemies I left behind.

Surely not the rice paddy where I lay bleeding, nor the blood-stained elephant grass where a medevac whirled me away.

I walked along the edge of Highway 1 as thousands of motorbikes rushed by: The new Vietnam, filled with young people, (70% under the age of thirty-five), with bright hopes and aspirations and an awakening belief in a better life.

I sat down by the roadside and wiped away silent tears, my face streaked with smoke, dust, and loss.

Trang Bang.

This is where we ordered villagers to squat down while we "searched and destroyed" their homes.

This is where Nick Ut photographed Phan Phuc, the "Napalm Girl", running naked down the highway, the sticky, gasoline flames burning her skin as she ran.

This is where Lonny, Baby San, Devil and I lay dying, dying not for God or flag or country, but simply because we were "the chosen", draftees offered up from poor black, brown, or white families by an upper-middle-class draft board that didn't want to take sons from their own.

I stood on the Trang Bang Bridge, gazed down from the railing, and saw my life drift by.

Like pages ripped out of "Life" or "Time", I saw my seventeen year-old wife's tattered face, Janice floating past on the rippling surface; I saw my mother's beat expression searching for her son.

Not far away, a film crew from Vietnam TV International recorded my anguish.

They came to follow my journey toward reconciliation, and have arranged a meeting with former members of The People's Army, soldiers who lived in Trang Bang and fought against me in 1968-69.

We sit at a table outside a government building and shook hands. At first, we were awkward, hesitant, reaching across the table to touch, clasp, and let go.

Our handshakes are strong, firm, the kind old soldiers give to compatriots from a distant war, but there is pain as well in our greeting.

Gone souls move under our eyes. We smile, but behind our smiles is heartache, sorrow, battles we didn't want but have to remember, shadows walking along the edges of our mouths.

I take out a map, and their fingers draw the lines along the borders of our youth.

"This is where your firebase was."

"This is where ten to twelve of us hid from you along the riverbank."

"This is the tunnel where our platoon slept by day and waited to attack you at night."

The television crew films our gestures, translates and captures the nuances of our despair.

Soon, there is nothing left to say.

We stand, awkwardly embrace, shake hands again, and say goodbye.

I am alone now, my journey done.

Tonight, in a Ho Chi Minh City hotel, I will write these final pages.

My reconciliation continues.

The legacy of leaving hundreds of thousands of unexploded bombs to kill more children; of fourth generation birth defects and genetic mutations caused by our massive spraying of Agent Orange--will not allow for my reconciliation.

All I can do is witness and tell, tell as I told the American public when I marched and protested as a member of the

Vietnam Veterans Against The War; tell as we told in the Winter Soldier hearings when we admitted to war crimes and atrocities.

So I tell.

And though there is no reconciliation for the dead, the bodies I counted and carried on my back these many years are gone, their spirits laid to rest.

Perhaps reconciliation is not an end, but a beginning, a healing process that starts with compassion and ends with grace.

Perhaps this is how angels are born from ghosts; angels whose wings are made of blood and bone; angels who live inside our imaginations and guide us by leaving testaments to truth.

I believe this book is such a testament, and hope these words are such a light.

May 1, 2015, Trang Bang, Vietnam
With love and gratitude to
Hoang Thu Trang, Le Hoang Linh,
and the many generous Vietnamese
friends who made this book complete,
r.g. cantalupo

In Shadow Before Light

I never heard the mortar call my name.

No one did.

Oh, maybe you heard the round shooting out the tube a thousand meters away, the muffled poomf! and then a buddy yelling "Incoming!", but once it was in the air, you never heard a sound.

If they were going to miss you, arc high over your head or to the left or right beyond you, then you might hear them spinning, a soft whistle like wind through bamboo as they spiraled past you through the sky.

If they were close though--close enough to wound or kill you, so close they were going to hit the ground only a few feet or a few inches from where you stood--you didn't hear a thing, you only saw the orange and red burst of the explosion, and felt the burning shrapnel tearing through your flesh.

But on this night, I heard nothing--neither the firing, nor the explosion.

We'd just returned from three weeks of 'search and destroy' in the Ho Bo Woods, and Firebase Pershing, the battalion headquarters, was a welcome sight, the place where hot showers, clean socks, warm meals, and letters from The World were waiting, where no L-shaped ambushes or hot LZ's lay around a bend in the trail or on the shadowy side of a tree line.

No, with two rings of concertina wire around the perimeter, four batteries of artillery, and the battalion command post dug in under three layers of sandbags, the firebase was relatively safe.

Only the occasional sniper from nearby rubber trees gave us the rush of terror now and then.

Or the sound of incoming mortars.

I awoke in the silent dark, not even the geckos cackling their favorite "fuck-you, fuck you, fuck you"; not even the crickets strumming their broken-stringed guitars.

I awoke and I did not know whether someone put a palm on my shoulder and nudged me, or whether some larger mystery roused me in the dark.

I awoke and the night was silent and I was inside a bunker, inside the belly of a beast whose rippled, olive-drab sandbag skin and steel ribs conjured up the belly of a gecko in my daze.

I doused my face with musty canteen water, tied my boot laces and stepped halfway into the doorway trying to find my bearings in the dark—

To the west nothing, not even a line where the horizon ended—

To the east, a few distant flares from a firefight too far to hear.

I turned toward the north, faced the perimeter our bunker guarded, and looked out into the night.

A red ember caught my eye.

One of the new guys on guard, smoking?

Dumb. Dumb. Really dumb. Sniper-bait.

You don't smoke out in the open at night. Not if you want to survive. Not if you want to keep your head. You have to hide it, shield it, cup the red ember wholly in your hands.

I step out of the doorway to tell him.

One step. Two. Three.

Time compressed into a rapid heartbeat and the rush of

adrenaline--toward the burning ember, deeper into the mouth of night.

From the moment I stepped through the dark doorway and into the open sky, I knew something was wrong.

Call it a premonition, a sixth sense, combat hyper-awareness, but as I stepped through the dark doorway into the naked sky, the hairs on the back of my neck spiked.

I felt like I was walking into the firing zone of an ambush just before the trip-wire snaps and the bombs explode.

I couldn't pinpoint it exactly, but I felt it.

It was too quiet maybe.

Or it was the careless red glow of the FNG's cigarette pinpointing our position.

Or it was the ominous black of the new-mooned night.

Call it what you want, but for the few seconds while the mortar was spinning toward me through the dark, I could feel death's breath on my neck.

One step. Two. Three.

Midway into the fourth, the ember burst into a thousand sparks.

I am blown into the night sky, thrown like a rag doll, a hundred burning fires shooting into my body as I hurl.

When I hit the ground, I hear someone screaming, "Medic!!! Medic!!!"—realize the voice is mine.

After that, all I remember is the heat, the red-hot metal, the jagged fragments piercing my arms, legs, chest, and head.

I remember the warm liquid oozing over my body, the jungle fatigues soaking and sticking to my skin, the dull throbbing, the fear flailing like a caged bird in the locked chambers of my heart.

Still, I do not remember how I got there.

Not then, and not now.

I don't remember whether I walked out of the bunker because someone roused me for guard duty, or if I'd simply wandered outside because I'd heard someone call my name.

Blood pours out my head, neck, chest, left arm and legs, drenching my jungle fatigues with a sticky wetness like warm pee.

I lay on my back, numb, the pain of my wounds not yet breaking through the shock of the explosion.

"Move!" I say to my body, "Crawl for cover!" but my body will not answer, my arms and legs beyond my words.

Blood seeps into the dry clay beneath me, forms a puddle like monsoon rain.

I am dissolving into the earth, sinking down in a warm pool.

Then a hand, hands start to pull me out, up. I see faces, flashlights with red lenses, red flames igniting my eyes.

I bounce up and down.

I am a huge insect with eight legs running toward a bunker.

I look up at the faces lit by red light.

I see fear, fear of death, fear of bad karma and bad luck, fear that whoever called to me may soon call to them.

And now I too am afraid, afraid of what they see, afraid of the bloody face reflected in their eyes.

"Hang in there, Radio!" Mike, our platoon leader, screams. "You're alright!"

His order will not rouse me. I can no longer hear his commands.

"How's the FNG?" someone asks.

"Gone. Mortar must've hit right where he was standing."

"You find a body for his tags?"

"Uhhh...no. Not much there, you know."

"Keep looking. Find something to tag. Alpha one, this is

Bravo-two-twelve. Request medevac. Affirmative. One. Yes, just one. Serious. How you doin', Ace?"

"I can't breathe."

"Medic!!! Where the fuck is that medic? Just relax, Radio, we'll have you out of here in ten minutes. You see the flash?"

"No."

"Nothing?"

"No…nothing."

I can't answer him. I can't talk. I want to sleep, close my eyes and sleep, let my body fall into that pit I've seen so many before me fall.

Besides, I didn't see the flash. The round must've already been in the air.

"I will not die here."

Others might, but not I.

I said it under my breath during lulls in firefights.

"I will not die here."

I said it as I walked out of the company's perimeter on eight-man night patrols deep into the terrifying jungle.

"I will not die here."

I said it as I lay on my back three hundred meters from the company's barb-wired perimeter on two-man listening posts as enemy soldiers moved in green shadows around us.

"I will not die here."

I said it as a promise, as a vow to myself against the war, as a pledge to my own allegiance.

I said it over and over to keep humping down the trail each day.

"I will not die…"

Not here.

Not in this god-forsaken country a world away from my wife and home.

Not here in this sick excuse for a war.

Not here where a life wasted is ever a bullet or trip wire away.

Not here.

Not now.

I said it after the mortar exploded and left me a crumpled heap on the ground.

I mouthed it in half-breaths.

"I will not die here."

I repeated it over and over like a mantra as I waited for the medevac to come.

"I will not die here."

I said it as I watched my buddies pull a poncho over the FNG's body parts.

I said it as blood pushed the air out of my punctured lung.

I said it as I looked at my reflection in Mike's eyes—a bloody, ripped face I've never seen.

I said it as I couldn't breathe.

"I will not die here."

I said it silently as I started to slip into irreversible shock from loss of blood.

"I will not die......

.here..."

Scissors cut through my bloody jungle fatigues, and quick fingers peel the pants and shirt apart to get at the wounds. Gauze bandages and tape are wrapped tightly around both my legs. Butterfly bandages pull the ragged gashes in my neck and head together. Compresses are taped to deep wounds in my left forearm and chest.

"I...I can't breathe, Doc."

"Okay. Let me get an I.V. in you."

"I'm fucked up ain't I, Doc?"

"You're alright. Just hold on, Radio. You're going back to The World. What's the ETA on the medevac?"

"Ten to fifteen." barked Mike.

"As soon as I get an I.V. in him and a chest tube, we need to run him down to the LZ."

I was down to half-breaths now, sips of air as if I were floating on my back in a turbulent sea. Waves jostled and broke over my head.

But the short gasps weren't enough. I needed more, more breath, more air, more than my collapsed lung could hold. I was hyperventilating, drowning in my own blood.

I close my eyes. The voices around me fade, and I drift into a peaceful half-sleep.

"I will not die here."

"Hey, Radio, wake the fuck up!"

I open my eyes as a needle pushes into my vein. An icy, burning liquid shoots through my right arm. My shirt is cut off and pulled away, and then a blade edge presses between two ribs. The blade pierces my skin sharply and stabs in. I can feel the metal inside me, but the pain is muted, far off, as if my punctured body were no longer mine. Through the numbness, I feel a tube slide through my ribs and into my chest. After a few minutes, the pressure on my lung begins to ease and I am able to breathe again.

"Alright, let's get him down to the LZ."

Mike, Lee, and a new guy pick up the stretcher while Doc holds the I.V. bag. Pain shoots through my wounds as they double-time me to the landing zone.

"I will not die here!"—but my voice is drowned out by the whirr of the rotor blades.

We rise slowly above Firebase Pershing, the olive drab entrails of the chopper like a cocoon around me, and out the doorway, the sparks of distant flares.

I know I need to stay conscious to survive, but my eyes slowly close, and the dark washes over me like black blood.

All I want to do is sleep, to let my body go.

Rotor blades chop through the heavy air. In the distance, I hear B-52's carpet-bombing the Ho Bo Woods—boom! boom! boom! boom! as the thousand pound bombs thud and explode against the wet earth.

Through the rotors' whirr, I hear the pilot's muffled voice talking to someone at the Army hospital in Chu Chi.

"Affirmative. One W.I.A. Multiple shrapnel wounds. That's affirm. Head, neck, chest, left arm, both legs. Grave. ETA about fifteen."

"Hey! Wake up, soldier! What's your name?"

The medic crouches over me and holds my face in his thick hands.

"Wha...?"

"I can't hear you! What's your name?"

"Radio."

"Okay, Radio, what's your mother's name?"

"What?"

"Your mother? Your mother? Open your eyes!!"

"Lil...Lillian."

"Where you from?"

"L.A."

"Alright Radio from L.A., you're not going to sleep on me are you?"

No answer. I'm back in that secret room behind my eyelids where the chopper's whirr and the medic's voice fade away.

No tunnel of white light to go through, no dead buddies and relatives waiting to greet me on the other side—nothing but a silent, dreamless sleep.

"I will not die..."

"I will not..."

"What company are you from?"

"How old are you?"

"How long have you been in country?"

His questions are staccato now, a rapid fire of question after question—rat-tat-tat-tat-tat-tat like a fifty caliber machine gun—meant to pull me back, to open the door to my secret room and pull me out.

"Wake up, Radio!"

I want to stay where I am, but I know if I stay here too long I will not return—"I will not die here."

I open my eyes to see the medic's face leaning over me, his green flight helmet starring down at me like a gigantic fly.

"Nineteen." I mutter. "Bravo."

There were no brain surgeons in Chu Chi.

The doctors and nurses who hovered over me with their tubes, clips, gauze, tape, and sutures stopped the bleeding from my neck, and the artery in my left arm.

They stabilized my heart rate and blood pressure and got me off the border between life and irreversible shock, but the more severe wounds, the shrapnel lodged in the membrane around my heart, repairing the vein severed at the juggler vein takeoff, and the two pieces of shrapnel somewhere inside my frontal lobe would have to wait.

The light where the horizon ended glowed like a red-hot machete's blade as I was wheeled out of the hospital doors and into another medevac.

I wanted to sleep now, to fall depthless into darkness, to slip out of my body, but the new medic wouldn't let me. He kept asking me the same tired questions as the chopper ascended into the lightening sky.

"What's your name?"

"Where are you from?"

"What company are you with?"

"What's your wife's name?"

The Earth's far edge was on fire, a slow burn eating the sphere's dark shadow as we rose above the hospital and then beyond the surrounding rice paddies and farms fringing the city.

We flew east into the blade of light, the chopper's whomp, whomp, whomp a comforting mantra as the flickering bursts of fire beneath us told another story, a story I would never be part of again.

And then I rose.

Above my body.

Above my life.

Is this my soul parting from my flesh, my spirit rising toward eternity, flying through the tunnel of white light toward people I loved?

I rose in darkness, in shadow, the body below me—my body—graying to a shade, the medic slowly dimming to a hazy silhouette.

I rose, but my wounds did not fly away on angel's wings, nor did I see my mortal life bleeding into light as if I were eternal.

I merely slipped in and out of a world filled with fire and burning pain—

--and then I fell.

Through the stretcher where I lay.

Through the olive-drab floor of the med-evac.

Through the black, night sky glittering with muzzle flashes and fiery explosions. Through the elephant grass and rice sprouts into the darker, moist earth below.

A silent falling, bodiless, weightless, like falling through the depths of a calm sea, like falling in a falling dream.

No sounds. No colors. No smells.

No faces of loved ones who'd passed on.

Nothing.

Just falling,

falling,

falling...

I fell as if I would fall forever, as if this life--our lives--from birth until death--was surrounded by this endless dark matter in which we all must fall.

Perhaps there is no heaven for soldiers, no realm beyond this world of blood and bone, no kingdom where the dying warrior rises into light.

Perhaps God departs from the battlefield as a spirit might depart, the air vibrating with His absence, the red rice paddies marked with His trail of blood.

Perhaps the tunnel of white light we all imagine is so blackened by the vestiges of war, that our souls remain on the Earth, staining our world like Hiroshima shadows silhouetting the walls of the city through Time.

For beyond the whomp, whomp, whomp of the medevac's swirling blades rising above or falling below my soul, I never heard God's voice summoning me back to life.

When my soul returned to the medevac, the only words I heard, came neither from a god nor an angel, but a man--green, insectlike in his helmet—his voice muted by whirling blades chopping through the heavy air, yelling—

"Wake up! Wake up, soldier! What's your name!? What's your name!? What's your name!?"

Somewhere between Chu Chi and Bien Hoa I surrendered.

I no longer fought my wounds, nor battled the medic's

interrogations to keep me awake.

I surrendered to the short, even breaths in syncopation with the steady beat of my heart, to the rock and roll movement of the med-evac as it rode the currents through the early morning twilight; to the jerk and tug and pull of more hands grabbing my stretcher and lifting me onto a gurney, and to the lights shooting by above me as I was rushed through the hallways and into another emergency room.

New doctors and nurses checked my wounds and reset the tubes and wires that hooked me up to machines, fluids, blood.

The bandages on my left arm were cut off and the wound re-examined. The butterfly sutures holding my neck wound closed were replaced by wire sutures. A fresh bag replaced the empty pint of blood dangling above my head. Then I was wheeled into the x-ray room to take pictures of my heart and brain.

Somewhere between the emergency room and the x-ray room, I surrendered to the realization I would survive, that I was no longer on the border between life and death, that I'd stopped floating between this and some other unknown realm.

After x-rays, I was wheeled into the pre-operation room where a neurosurgeon spoke to me about the upcoming craniotomy he would perform.

"Hello. I'm Doctor Chang."

I looked at him with dead eyes.

"We're going to have to do some surgery to remove a few pieces of shrapnel from your brain."

I didn't say anything.

"You have two small fragments in your frontal lobe area. We have to remove them."

I was lucid then, clear.

"What are my chances?"

Doctor Chang held my stare, then smiled.

Not a fake smile he put on to diminish my trepidation, but a genuine smile created out of the directness of my question.

Here I was, a nineteen year old kid with wounds all over his body, a young soldier who'd been medevaced out of the bush a little over three hours earlier, asking whether I would live or die at his hand.

And so my sheer audacity, my black and white innocence broke through his professional demeanor

He smiled and patted my good arm.

"You're going to be just fine soldier."

And, for that one small moment, I believed him.

I lay in the pre-operation room as drops of anesthesia dripped through the IV tube into my bloodstream, and I slowly slipped away.

Not falling or rising, but floating, drifting inside the deepest sleep I've ever known—a sleep not unlike death perhaps, if there is a likeness to death in life.

Limbo.

Somewhere between heaven and hell.

Around me the sound of tools whirred, the vague tones of voices, the metallic clink and clatter of instruments—a dull buzz, buzz, buzz as my hair was shaved off, soft rasps as a razor cut the stubble from my skull until there was nothing, the smooth surface of skin and the crushed right forehead where the shrapnel smashed through my skull--a scalpel, a serrated blade, a pinchers and a clamp to pull and hold the cranial flap open and peel the skin off the skull.

And then there were more voices, close, closer to my ear—the surgeon and his nurses—and other sounds—the electric whirr of the saw cutting through my skull, the I.V.'s drip, drip, drip pulling me out into an endless sea—the odor of blood, the tincture of anesthesia and antiseptic—drifting out, out, out, floating on the waves...

...and somewhere...drifting out to sea...

I awoke.

The sounds of the hospital returned.

Gurney wheels rolled past where I lay.

There was a cry, a muffled moan, a doctor's voice calling for a compress, a clip, a nurse running by.

In the far, far distance, explosions, the heavy, slow, rat-tat-tat of fifty caliber machine guns, the call and response of mortars, rockets and artillery rounds...

I woke in a room, a bed, at some indeterminable time, night, yes, surely night, or early morning, no light coming through the bamboo blinds, and yet I was still drifting, floating on a raft, floating in blackness on a dark, uncharted sea.

I tried to lift my arms, but I could not.

I tried to shift my hips, move my legs, turn, sit up, rise, but I could not.

I cannot feel my body, my face, my skin. I cannot open my mouth to call.

I do not know if I breathe, if I am breathing, if I am still alive...

I drift.

Through darkness. Through space.

In the distance, I hear the whirr of a saw as it cuts through my skull.

I drift. And drift. And drift.

And when I awaken again there is light, not white light, but a surgeon's lights; not the light of eternity, but the light of life, the light where shadows end.

In Light Before Shadow

"Cantalupo? Where you from?"

"L.A."

"How 'bout I call you Cantaloupe for short."

"Cantaloupe's fine, sarge."

"You know much about radios? PRC-25s?"

"No."

"How 'bout point? You wanna walk point?"

"Point?"

"We need a point man and an RTO. Your choice. You look like a radio man to me."

"Yeah?"

"You've got a good back. You lift weights?"

"I played football in high school. Was a wrestler in college."

"A college man, huh? What the fuck you doin' in the 'Nam?"

"Draft board. Came from the wrong side of town, I guess."

"Good thing you ain't black. They woulda drafted your father and your brother too. Me, I love this shit. Nobody fucks with you once you know the rules. Gonna re-up for another four when this one's done. Get to be Master Sergeant someday."

"I heard RTO's don't last long."

"They tell you all kinda shit in A.I.T. (Advanced Infantry Training). Radio man lasts longer than point. But it's all relative, my man. When the shit starts flying, it's all fuckin relative."

"Relative to what?"

"Relative to the shit. Some companies don't hit the shit for months. Just hump through the boonies like they were walking on water. The 25th, especially the 2ndBattalion, we hit the shit nearly every day. If it ain't a sniper, it's a booby trap. If it ain't a booby trap or a sniper, it's a mortar or an RPG attack. And if it ain't none of those, it's a hot LZ or a U-shaped ambush or a full-on fucking gook assault."

"You're short though? Heard you only have a couple months to go."

"Short? Fuck, you ain't short till you kiss the ground you were born on. Last month a C-140 loaded with short-timers heading back to The World took a direct hit from a rocket while it was taxiing on the tarmac at Ton Son Nhut. No, short don't mean shit until you're gone, man. I'm not short. I'm lucky. And I'm gonna stay lucky."

Lee pulled out his dog-tag chain from his neck. An AK-47 bullet was strung through the chain beside the black-taped, camouflaged dog-tags.

"You see this? This is my lucky charm."

"An AK bullet?"

"Yeah. Had my name on it but couldn't say it out loud. Went through an M-16 magazine, hit the smoke canister strapped around my chest, and lodged in my flak jacket. So now it's my lucky charm. Being short don't mean nothin. It means I've made it through 243 days without getting wasted. It means there ain't another ten guys in this company that made it through to 244. But in the big scheme of things, only this bullet matters. First thing you gotta do is get you a lucky charm. So...point or radio?"

"Radio."

"Alright Radio, you're Mike's bitch. You follow him around

like stink on shit. He calls, you gotta get to where he is. You gotta low-crawl through machinegun fire, mortars, RPG's exploding over your head, AK's ripping through the rice paddy berms you're crouched behind—I don't give a fuck. That's your job. You don't get to Mike, Mike don't call in support, Mike don't tell the C.O. what the fuck's going on, and then the whole platoon's fucked. You're our mouth and ears. And you know what happens when you're deaf and dumb don't you?"

"No, not really."

"We cut off your fuckin head and mount it on a Punji Stick."

"Maybe I shoulda picked point."

"Listen, you forget about all that shit you heard in The World. This aint The World, this is the bush. And in the bush, shit happens. There ain't no reason for how it happens, or when it happens, or if it's gonna be the same shit that happened yesterday or the same shit that's gonna happen tomorrow. You do your job and you stick beside me or Mike or one of the other guys who's seen the shit and if you're lucky you'll survive. That's all you gotta know."

"He go home?"

"Who?"

"The one I'm replacing?"

"Home? Yeah. He went home."

"So he made it?"

"He didn't make shit, man. Another college boy. Thought he was too smart for the fuckin boonies. Had a bad attitude. Didn't listen to nobody. Sat out in the open with his antenna waving in the sky like a fuckin flag, cookin Ham N' Eggs. Sniper took half his jaw off while the spoon was still in his mouth. Didn't last a fuckin month. Now here's your radio. You make sure you don't fuck up."

Yeah, Lee owned a smile wide as a crescent moon, but, when it came to the war, he was all business, his eyes cold as polished coal, his deep, black skin caked with camouflage paste and mud.

He rarely spoke about home, or Indiana, or the small town outside Indianapolis where his family lived.

He didn't carry a picture of his girlfriend or his family.

He never told anyone why he enlisted, why he volunteered to be a "Shake N' Bake" (an Instant NCO), or if there was anyone he loved back in The World.

Like most of the guys I got to know in Bravo Company, once the bush took root inside you, it grew wild like bamboo. Before long, it blocked out the window of the world you once remembered. The war was all that mattered, humping through this day and the next and the next till your year was over, your life reprieved, and you rose up from the tarmac to begin again.

So I became an R.T.O., a radio operator for the weapons platoon in Bravo Company, 2ndof the 12thBattalion, 4thBrigade of the 25thInfantry Division.

When I was a kid, I loved listening to Dodger baseball games on the radio. I would spend hours listening to Vince Sculley calling the play by play.

But as a radio operator, I listened to the sounds of firefights, to the play by play of terrified soldiers fighting to survive.

Like any other soldier in Bravo Company, I could look out from the high ground of Fire Support Base Pershing and see the war going on for miles. I could see the flashes of bombs exploding at the end of the dark horizon, pounding the rubber trees of the Ho Bo Woods into volcano-like craters, hear the staccato thumping of thousand-pounders like a stampede of Tyrannosaurs, and feel the rumble beneath me as if an earthquake rolled over the rice paddies.

But unlike other combat soldiers, I not only saw the green and white tracers of a battle arcing across the sky, I listened to the firefights burning through the voices of the grunts who are there.

I bore witness.

I could hear the terror, the chaotic commands, the cries of pain and the calls for fire support and medevacs.

I could imagine the bullets and shrapnel tearing through bone and flesh as explosions went off around them.

But I could not help.

I could not fire my M-16 on the waves of enemy soldiers that crawled closer toward them, nor bandage the sucking chest wounds that devoured their breath.

And when the squelch and static died, I knew the man on the other end of the receiver was wounded or dying and I might be the last to hear.

I never believed in fate.

I never believed what happens happens because it was meant to be as if I were simply filling in the pages of my already written life's story.

I never believed the stray bullet or the booby-trapped bomb was up ahead on the trail somewhere waiting with my name.

No, if I believed in anything it was luck.

Hard luck and lucky runs. The yin and yang of happenstance.

Chaos and random disasters.

Luck wasn't always my religion.

When I first graduated from high school, I imagined my life as an endless adventure.

I was going to head out, hitch-hike across country, lose myself in the body of America, disappear like Sal Paradise in On The Road into some romantic vision of myself.

But then reality hit me like a lightening bolt.

Six months after graduation, during the Christmas holidays, my sixteen-year old girlfriend and I fumbled through our virginity. Two months later, we found out she was pregnant.

We got married in April, and I took a job at Pacific Bell Telephone delivering company mail.

I envied Sal Paradise, but The Road would have to wait.

Somewhere in my mind's far reaches there were shadows: vague shapes of soldiers running ragged through prime time news, flag-wrapped coffins returning with the bodies of high school friends, my best buddy Wayne, a Canadian citizen, getting classified 1-A.

And though I didn't know much about war, nor care for the causes and justifications, I knew if this one went on long enough, I would have to face it, stare it down like the demon that it was.

I was barely eighteen at the time, but I was eligible for the draft.

It wasn't fate.

But it was very bad luck.

We prayed to Elephant, to the God of Charmed Ears, to the God of Rock n' Roll.

We prayed for Snoopy, for Puff the Magic Dragon, for the Phantoms to rain down fire at 1000 rounds a minute.

We prayed for the gift of crossing off another day, for the courage to hump one day closer to home, for our M-16s never to jam, for our claymore mines to explode when the enemy was close, for our flares to light the dark ground where ghostly soldiers crawled through the elephant grass.

We prayed, and even a shark's tooth from the Pacific Ocean owned the power to save us.

Or no power at all.

And when Elephant, and Saint Christopher, and Jesus, and Charmed Teeth, and Jacks and Aces, and all our words didn't save us anymore; when the many gods we've created in this world were blown to kingdom come, when a trip-wired grenade exploded beneath a buddy's legs, or a gut wound gushed blood and intestines, or a punctured lung sucked on the night's dead air; when the enemy broke through and overran our perimeter, or our M-16s jammed at the moment our lives most depended on them; when the jets arrived too late, or the artillery rounds landed too short and rained down upon us; when all our prayers died in the godless jungle and unhallowed paddies, then all the gods we'd created lost their power and we cursed them, we cursed them and swore off all that was consecrated but our selves.

God became a nickname in a letter, a flag-wrapped coffin, the last snapshot home—

God became a dooby, a toot, a chug, whatever soothed the shakes and the night terrors and let the good sleep come—

God became movement, flux, limbo, the endless patrol, time's executioner, a prisoner locked in the unknown soldier's tomb—

And, when there was no god left to save us, no god left to pray to, no god beyond I, I alone, I forsaken, I slipped deeper into darkness, deeper into the war.

Hump.

Stop.

Hump.

Down a road. Along a trail. Across a bridge. Into a village. Trang Bang. Four clicks and back. Thirty miles northeast of Saigon.

Hump. Stop. Hump.

To Trang Bang and back. Along Highway 1. 9/1/68.

The heat kills. The PRC-25 radio cuts into my shoulder blades. The hundred plus pounds I carry sinks me ankle deep in monsoon mud.

I carry forty M-16 magazines over my shoulder each loaded with nineteen rounds.

I carry four grenades, four canisters of smoke--yellow, orange, red, green--two claymore mines, one red-lensed flashlight.

I carry one poncho liner and one waterproof poncho to lay over the wet earth or to keep the monsoon rain from drenching me.

I carry two canteens of stale, tepid water, three pairs of olive-drab socks, a first aid kit of bandages, gauze, and a large waterproof patch for sucking chest wounds.

I carry "The World" in a waterproof plastic bag to keep safe from the sweat, blood and rain: Letters from my wife, my mother, my buddy Wayne in the 101stAirborne, photos from home.

I carry God: A Saint Christopher dances over my chest strung on a dog-tag chain, a crucifixion bobs in the sweat band of my steel pot where my third eye used to be.

I carry Luck: A shark's tooth, a rattler's rattle, my graduation ring strung through a necklace of love beads.

I carry a week's worth of C's: Ham n'eggs. Spaghetti and meat balls. Meat loaf and beef stew. Peanut butter and jelly. Pound cake. Peaches. Coffee and heat tabs.

Later, one pound cake and one can of peaches (my favorite) will be worth two peanut butters or two ham n' eggs in trade. To Devil. To Baby San. To Spike. (Devil says the peaches give him the runs.)

Later, I will pour the golden slices over pound cake, mix in a packet of powdered milk for my coffee. Eat peaches and pound cake in C-ration heaven.

Later.

On another day.

But not today.

Not now.

Now, I simply hump.

Hump. Stop. Hump.

Read the earth, the trees, the sky.

Watch for trip wires.

Watch for snipers.

Watch for booby traps, punji-sticked holes, the distant flash of incoming mortars.

Watch for a leaf's twitter, a cricket's broken guitar, a fuck-you lizard's silence, a palm-sized scorpion skittering across the trail.

Watch for hot LZs, for bamboo-covered spider holes, for the blue-steel glint of an AK-47's snout poking through bamboo, for a U-shaped ambush waiting round the bend.

Watch for signs, warnings, premonitions, a sudden rush of bad vibes.

Watch for enemies in black pajamas running through shadowed brush.

Watch and listen and wait.

And hump.

The heat kills. The straps of the PRC-25 radio bite into my shoulder blades like an army of fire ants.

I am nineteen.

I am immortal.

"I will not die here."

I stagger drunkenly down the trail.

The intermittent squelch of the radio; the jagged line of lumbering green-fatigued bodies; the close and distant sounds of war.

I am nineteen.

I will not die here. I will not die…here. I will not…die…

here.

The heat kills.

The PRC-25 eats my shoulder blades.

A new guy drops and disappears in the elephant grass.

Another, humping along on flank, collapses in the high brush, his brain simmering over, his eyes boiled and rolled backward in his head like pale white eggs.

An M-60 machine-gunner humping ten meters ahead of me staggers and falls, the hammer of too much heat striking him down, the orange ball of the sun pressed against his forehead like the ball end of a sledge.

"Where the fuck is the left flank?" the company commander yells. "Where's the Pillsbury boy?" What the fuck happened to the FNG?"

Then someone will be sent to find him, or them—the flank or the FNG or the M-60 gunner who is no longer ten meters ahead—and that someone will find him, spot him lying face down in the clay, roll him over, see his eyes peeled back till only the whites show, his face pale blue, his skin the gray-white of ash.

Someone will find him, and that someone will yell "Medic! Medic!" and then a medic will run out to where the collapsed man lies, fix an injection of adrenalin, an I.V. of electrolytes, fluids, ask the company commander to call for a med-evac, hope he can keep him alive till it arrives.

Hump.

Stop.

Hump.

An orange flame in the sky torches our brains, ignites a

white-hot blaze that turns our bodies cold.

The heat kills. The straps of the radio cut through my flesh. Sweat streams down my face in rivulets of dirty tears.

Hump.

Stop.

Hump.

I stagger as I walk, the weight too much to bear.

I want to throw it off.

I want to quick-release this war and drop it right where I am.

I want to tear off my jungle fatigues and run away from this jagged line of green.

I want the rest of my 349 days to be done. Over.

Now.

Right fucking now.

I hump the trail slowly, warily, looking and stopping, listening and waiting, crossing Trang Bang Bridge heading for the village, heading for checkpoint Charlie, ready to engage, ready to search and destroy, ready to call in Phantoms, 155's, five-hundred pound bombs, ready to call for "Snoopy" or "Puff, the Magic Dragon", or Cobras, whatever we need to waste, destroy, to wipe out the enemy before the enemy wipes out us.

And today is a good day.

No one will die—not from the heat, or from a booby trap, or from a sniper.

A battalion of Viet Cong fire ants will not attack my head and neck as my antenna strikes the branch where they nest.

No, that will happen on another day, on other days, but not today.

Today, I will be new and the country will lay itself out new before me in a dress of emerald and tan, gold rhinestones of sun flashing off the surface of the rice paddies in the distance, the sky bluer than a robin's egg, the radio breaking and squelching as I walk, the muted sounds of far off battles, AK's and M-16's in a deadly dialogue, gun-ships raking stands of trees, two Phantoms tearing the fabric of the sky--stopping and starting, starting and stopping, looking for booby traps, trip-wires, spider-holes, caches, snipers, a battalion of NVA--stopping and starting, searching and destroying, crossing into the village, heading for checkpoint Charlie—

—And then a single explosion.

Muffled.

Ahead.

Somewhere near the front of our line.

And everyone will dive down, adrenalin pumping for the imagined firefight to begin.

I am too far away from the explosion to know what happened, but the radio tells all: A Viet Cong guerilla, a homemade booby-trap, the point man blown up as he entered the village, less than ten meters away from the blast.

I hear the point man's moans on the radio as the C.O. calls for a med-evac.

Hump.

Stop.

Hump.

Hear and hear and hear.

The point man's moans. The CO's calls. The medic's questions. The wounded man's answers to stay alive.

Hear, and witness, and wait.

Sit down in the dense, sweltering shade of a rubber tree. Light a free Malboro. Smoke. Take two swigs from my canteen.

Wait till the order comes down to "saddle up, move on,"

head out toward check point Charlie.

Someone says, "one week and a wakeup, one week and a wake up and I'm gone."

Someone else says, "fuck you, Dog. I heard you like it here so much, you re-upped for another tour."

"Yeah, I be here alright, I be here when the 'Nam freezes over and there ain't nothin' but boom boom girls to keep me warm."

I watch the line of resting bodies awaken, pull backpacks back on, stagger drunkenly to stand.

I put the straps back on my shoulders, but I cannot rise. The weight of the radio and 100-pound-plus pack is too much. I struggle and tip over like a tipped over cow. I try again. A few short-timers laugh.

"Fucking-new-guy," like a chorus of harpies.

I roll my hips sideways, get one leg under, then the other, squat, shift, lift, wobble drunkenly to my feet.

I am a pack animal now, mule or water-buffalo, lumbering down Highway 1, in line with the others.

About a hundred meters or so up the road, in the makeshift shade of a lean-to, a wounded man lays--the point-man--and a few meters ahead, his enemy, a boy of about eight or nine.

This is our enemy? This boy? This Viet Cong? But how can that be? How can he the ones we are supposed to kill?

I pass by the point man, a bloody gauze bandage wrapped around his head and eyes, a black kid, maybe twenty, blood splashed over his jungle fatigues, a medic talking to him, asking him questions, trying to keep him from falling into shock, "What's your name, soldier? Where you from? Where you from?"

I pass by the boy-Cong.

He is terrified, but his face is stone, cold, empty.

I don't see a mother in his eyes.

I don't see a brother, a sister, a father, a family.

I see the dead.

I see grief, rage, a heart empty as a black hole.

I pass into the village, Trang Bang, Vietnamese peasants squatting down, waiting for us to pass.

The heat kills, as do the snipers, the booby-traps, the mortars, the RPGs, the hot LZs, the L and U-shaped ambushes, the bright, lightening-quick, coral snakes, the huge, tail-waving black scorpions, the dense and impenetrable jungle.

Hump.

Stop.

Hump.

The day done.

I, no longer 19, no longer green, no longer young.

Between the squelches and the staccato bits of information, between the calls for more firepower and the calls for med-evacs, I have learned the sounds—the groans and the terrors, the chaos and the hurried orders—the desperate voices, the explosions, the bursts of fire, the whole, fucking grotesque, bone-work of the war.

I vomited the first time I saw what a 500 pound bomb does to a man.

We'd chased two suspected Viet Cong for an hour through the rice paddies. When they ran into a hootch to hide, the C.O. requested a strike.

The Phantom circled around once and streaked low for the drop. Sighted in, a bomb fell out of the jet's belly and jettisoned toward the hooch. Upon impact, flames, smoke, and debris burst up into the turquoise sky.

When the smoke and debris cleared, the hooch was gone, the two men vanished. The C.O. sent my platoon in to see if they were alive. Baby San, the point, was the first in, second was Mike, our platoon leader, then I, not far behind with the radio.

The thatched embers smoldered and hissed under our boots as we snaked closer. Spike and Devil poked through the ashen debris till they found the hole where the two men hid. I was about ten meters away from the rubble when I heard a faint groan. One of the men was still alive.

There wasn't much left of their bodies and what was left looked like the skinned torsos of slaughtered cows. I'd never seen a human body look like that. A run over dog lying on a road side looked better. A bloody turkey with its head twisted from its neck looked less grotesque.

So I puked. I felt the nausea rising up from my stomach and barfed.

Right there. Right in the middle of the smoldering ashes and bits of flesh.

No one said anything. Mike turned his head away from the ruined bodies, took in my hunched over torso, then turned back to the dying guerilla as Spike pulled what was left of him out of the debris.

When I was done puking, Mike called me over, took the phone from the PRC-25 and called back to the C.O.

If this were a rite of passage, I'd passed through to the other side.

If this was where we were going, we were not coming back.

"You gotta love this war," mused Spike, panning his M-60 across to a water buffalo lumbering through the elephant grass.

"You really get off on this shit, don't you Spike?"

"You don't?"

"It is what it is." Devil surveyed the bombed out ruins of a pagoda and picked up a dusty fragment of a stone Buddha. "It is what it is."

"Yeah, last night this was a black dot on a grid, a fuckin' speck. And now—"

"And now it's a fuckin' crater."

"I swear, I think you love these gooks, Radio."

"I respect them. There's a difference. You don't respect shit, Spike."

"I got all the respect I need right here." Spike lock and loaded his M-60 machinegun and panned it across the horizon. He again stopped on the water buffalo grazing about a hundred meters away.

"Impressive, ain't it?" Lonny posed.

"What?" asked Lee.

"Seeing what 20 82's fired for effect can do."

"Just a speck on a map, man. Just a speck on a map in a shithole country in a shithole war. You see any blood trails?"

"Nobody crawled away from this shit, Spike. Not even Buddha." Devil put the stone fragment in his pocket and nudged some debris with the muzzle of his M-16.

"Let the water buffalo be, Spike. We're here to check out the pagoda, not start a war with dumb animals."

"Could be a Viet Cong water buffalo, Sergeant."

"I said, let it to fuck be!"

Mike came up behind Lee and gestured toward Spike who was moving out toward the field.

"What's John Wayne up to this time?"

"Dumb fuck wants to waste a water buffalo," shot Lee. "If he had more than shit for brains, he'd be dangerous."

"He's already dangerous. Thinks he's in a fuckin' war movie."

"Hey Spike, Mike says you think you're John Wayne in

'The Green Berets'." roared Devil.

"Keep your voice down, you'll wake the dead."

"You got that right, Devil, I am in a fuckin' war movie!" Spike shot back.

"If you don't keep your traps shut, I'm gonna put you in my war movie!" ripped Mike. "Nothin' worse than a fucking FNG with a hard on for war. Spike, get your ass back here, you're sniper bait out there by your lonesome."

Spike lumbered back and put his M-60 at rest.

"You get your shit together or I'm gonna volunteer you for permanent night patrol.

"I didn't mean no harm, Sergeant, just wanted a little pay back after—"

"First off, out here I'm no sergeant. I'm nobody. I'm Mike. You leave all that rank shit back in the base camp. I don't need some sniper thinking I'm in charge."

"Sorry. I didn't think--"

"That's because you've got shit between your ears. How long you been in the bush? A month?"

"Twenty-four days. Today's twenty-five."

"That's twenty-four days longer than you need to be John Wayne in the 'Green Berets'. This ain't no place for heroes. Here, all the heroes are dead, and if they ain't dead, they're getting other people killed. You be a hero out here, and you're gonna end up with a bullet between your blue eyes."

"I wasn't—"

"You believe in God?"

"I'm a Baptist."

"Than get this 'Spike the Baptist'. I don't know what brainless fuck over at Battalion Headquarters gave us these coordinates for H & I's, but we don't need to be fuckin' with somebody else's god. It's bad luck. And wasting that water buffalo is bad luck too."

"Uh…I—"

"You pray?"

"What do you mean?"

"Lee says you carry a bible."

"I like to keep one with me, yes."

"Good. Then you pray for us. You pray this fuckin' dismembered Buddha here forgives us for blowin' his temple all to shit."

"But—"

"That's a fuckin' order. You pray to your God to tell their god this was a mistake. You got that?"

"Yes. I got it."

"Now get your gear together, we're moving up the road in five."

Mike headed off beyond the pagoda to survey the horizon. Smoke spiraled up from a stand of banyan trees. He panned across the rice paddies and the trees, then walked back.

Spike and the rest of us got our gear together.

"Superstitious motherfucker, ain't he?" spit Spike.

"After two tours, you get superstitious or you get dead," fired Lee.

"What you carry a bible for anyway? Ain't you got enough weight with that M-60?" asked Devil.

"God lightens my load."

"You gotta be fuckin' kiddin' me. Pscho-killer's a god-damn Jesus freak?"

"He's a freak alright," jabbed Lonny, "a stone cold head case freak."

"Yeah, with God on his side." barked Mike as he returned. "Let's move out. I'll be expecting a good prayer."

"I can't pray without my bible."

"When we get to the checkpoint, you make sure he takes it out, Lee."

"Affirmative!"

"Spike, get behind point. Let's move!"

"Fuckin' freak," spit Devil.

"Yeah, a mothafuckin' Jesus freak."

"With shit for brains."

Devil and Lonny were my best friends.

At Pershing, Lonny and I shared a two-man bunker. He slept on one side, I, the other. Devil lived in the bunker adjacent to us with Lee.

There wasn't anything particularly unusual about this set-up, except that I was white, and Lonny, Devil, and Lee were black, and this was 1968, three years after the war was no longer a "police action", seven month's after Martin Luther King's assassination, five month's past Bobby Kennedy's, four month's after the country erupted in race riots all across America, and less then a year into the current average of 50,000 draftees per month—mostly blacks, Hispanics, and poor whites—being inducted into the Army and Marines.

Vietnam--a reflection of the fissure in the United States between white and black, rich and poor, the haves and the have-nots--was a booby trap ready to explode if anyone hit the fine filament of the trip-wire called racism.

And, by bunking with Lonny, by Devil and Lonny being my best friends--I put myself right in the crosshairs of racism's killing zone.

Lonny and I came to the bush together. We were both from California, both high school athletes, both draftees against the war. We'd both grown up poor, raised by single mothers.

Lonny was wiry, lean, not a pound of fat anywhere. His

eyes were a shade darker than my own.

I was his opposite. I was husky, short, strong as a pack animal, built for carrying, whereas Lonny's body was built for running. His skin was smooth, unblemished, the color of mahogany.

My skin turned olive-brown in the Vietnam sun.

So though our skin colors were shades apart, our life experiences and interests were similar.

Besides, we were the FNG's for our first month until more FNG's arrived, and that bound us.

We were sent out on two man listening posts together and eight man night patrols. We got the shit details together. He poured gasoline into fifty galloon drums while I lit the pungent stew of toilet paper, excrement, and piss, and stirred the soupy shit into flames.

Getting assigned the same bunker in Firebase Pershing was fine with us. We celebrated our first C-ration dinner in our bunker by promising to survive the year together, each covering the other's back when the shit got bad.

Spike, a red-neck from Arkansas, hated that I lived with a black man. He thought it was somehow sacrilegious, a blasphemy to the white Aryan race. Oh, it was okay to be side by side with a "nigger" in a firefight, to be in the same foxhole together when all hell breaks loose—blood running the same color and all—but living in the same bunker together threatened Spike's notion of being white.

Out in the bush, in a firefight—black or white—brown or red—was just another face behind a weapon, but back in the base camp, red-necked whites and black power blacks clustered together, gathered in bunkers to talk shit about the other.

The red-necked good ole' boys thought Lonny and I were just faggots from California, and for the black power blacks my being white living with a black crossed some imaginary color barrier in their mind, or somehow diminished the power in their black fist.

I didn't give a shit.

I didn't like fist pumping black apostles of hate anymore than red-necks.

I was a product of the tenements and saw the war as an equal opportunity killer, everyone wallowed in the same shit, and the enemy didn't care if your skin color was pink or camouflage-green.

So I didn't see Lonny's shit, piss, sweat and blood any different than my own.

After three weeks in the bush he stank the same as I. The jungle rot between his toes looked as pink and raw as mine and smelled like the same green mold. And all that bullshit about black cocks being bigger than white's was put to rest one night when Devil, Lonny, and I got drunk and decided to have a contest.

I had an inch at least on Lonny, and my cock was thicker, but Devil put us both to shame.

I wasn't surprised. Devil was a big man. He was 6'2" and weighed over two-hundred fifty pounds. His thighs, biceps, head, neck, and yes, cock, were almost double the size of either Lonny's or mine. Black had nothing to do with it, bigness did.

Because Devil, Lonny and I hung out together there were rifts on both sides of the color divide.

Spike called me a nigger lover. He never said that to my face, but I heard the whispers and snickers as I passed by his bunker on his red-neck beer and poker nights at Pershing. The red-neck white bunkers seemed to be situated close to each other, four or five with Southern and Mid-Western whites bunkered together. Boys from Idaho and Montana, dumb as cows. Some came from rural towns whose only contact with a black man might have been in a high school football game, and were mostly followers. They were more ignorant than racist, but with someone like Spike instigating, they could be just as bad as their granddaddy's in a white hood.

Out in the field, prejudices slipped under the mask of fear and hyper-vigilance, but in Pershing, the masks came off as the pot and beer came on. Rumors, petty gossip, prejudices flew like incoming mortars. And by late 1968 there was a lot of shit flying around both real and imagined.

Spike came up to me one afternoon after we'd come back from the Ho Bo Woods.

"I hear you're a darkie like your buddies."

"What the fuck does that mean?"

"I don't care mind you, darkie's and creole's all the same to me. I fucked a creole from Louisiana once. Best piece of ass I ever had. She was just a shade darker than you but was still half-nigger blood."

"I'm Sicilian if that's what you mean. A lot of Sicilian's have black blood in their family history. Black Sicilian's we call them."

"What the fuck is a Black Sicilian?"

"Means we have Moor blood running through our veins."

"More than what?"

"Moors. Black Arabs. Sicily was ruled by Moors for a couple of hundred years."

"Is that why some of you Wops have kinky hair?"

"I'm Sicilian, not Italian. And we don't have frizzy hair. We have curly hair."

"But these black Arabs were niggers weren't they?"

"Only you dumb motherfuckers call people niggers. We call the Moors Moors."

"What the fuck is that supposed to mean?"

"Means the only niggers I see are white."

"Niggers don't have white skin."

"Niggers come in all colors, but mostly they come in white skin with Southern drawls like they have shit in their mouth when they talk. And there's only one thing all niggers have in common, Spike. They are all fucking dumb. They look in the mirror and see God's children and don't realize God ain't as fucking dumb as their stupid faces. Niggers are so fucking dumb they forget God only had one child and he was a Jew."

"Yeah, well where I come from you're a nigger. You live with niggers. You smell like a nigger. And one day you're gonna die like a nigger."

"Watch your back, Spike. One day that M-60 might jamb on you and you're gonna need a nigger like me to save your nigger ass."

Baby San was seventeen when he joined the Army. Now nineteen, with the same baby-faced looks as when he'd joined, he was a sergeant, a veteran of five months in the field. Only his tired blue eyes, dishrag blond hair, and a face ever-streaked with camouflage paste and mud, gave him the hardened edge of a veteran, his eyes swimming in the dark pools of what he'd already seen and experienced, sinking deeper in their sockets than the eyes of any twenty year lifer.

He was the one who ultimately told all FNG's about "Smiles" and the history of Bravo Company, 2/12 Battalion, 25thInfantry Division.

I met "Smiles" in the back of a deuce and a half returning from Chu Chi.

An unlit cigarette hung from his bottom lip. His eyes were dead as coal.

"You want a light."

He didn't look at me. He simply took the zippo with my hand, lit his cigarette, and jumped out of the truck bed heading toward the CP bunker.

"What's with him," I asked Baby San, as I watched him walk away, puffs of smoke floating up behind him as he disappeared.

"He's shot, man. I don't know what he's doing back here. He was shot the morning he walked out of the Ho Bo Woods."

"He was one of the six?"

"He led them out, took command after the officers and platoon leaders went down."

"Must've been one hell of a firefight," Lonny chimed in.

"Hell. No. Hell's just got flames and demons. That day the Ho Bo rained napalm and 500 pound bombs, M-16s melted into steel pots and crucifixions, charred and twisted bits of metal and flesh. You couldn't tell a dog tag from a Saint Christopher after the Phantoms were done."

"They called jets in on themselves?"

"Had to. They were overrun, cut off from the rest of the company. It was either that or let the NVA have them. Half of them were already dead or dying. No, my brothers, hell's got nothing on that day."

No one seemed to know what happened to 'Smiles' after the day he walked off headed toward the Command Post.

Someone said he got killed that night on night patrol.

Someone else said he left the Fire Support Base and ended up in Long Binh Prison, a deserter.

Baby San said he was sent to Ton Son Nhut Air Base to serve the rest of his tour, hanging out at the bars with boom-boom girls at night and surfing during the day.

I wanted to believe he went home, back to his wife and family.

I wanted to believe he was alive.

We lumbered along a thin trail the NVA and Viet Cong used to run supplies and set up ambushes, but sometimes we lost the trail and the only way on was with machetes.

Dirty sweat streamed down our foreheads and glazed our skin. We hacked through the wait-a-minute vines and bamboo thickets, past palm fronds larger than a man. Sometimes the machetes slipped out of our hands mid-swing and swished into the thick brush. One FNG lost his machete in the tall elephant grass and Mike made him low-crawl into the brush till he found it.

We worked in tandem, one man scything till his arms went numb or his brains boiled inside his steel pot and the next would take over while the first splashed tepid canteen water over his head to cool down.

"Take five."

We dropped our backpacks where we stood and slid our canteens out for a drink of warm water.

Devil flicked his Marlboro and blew smoke up into the dark green canopy. "They ought to kill all this shit. Spray it and burn it till there ain't nothing left but blue ashes."

"You can't kill everything," said Baby San.

"Why not? It's just a fuckin jungle," Spike spit.

"So you want to defoliate the whole fuckin bush?"

"If there weren't no bush there wouldn't be no bush to hide in."

"They'd go underground. You want to chase them out of spider holes day and night."

"Be better than chasing them through this jungle. Yeah, I'd turn this shit into a parking lot, if it made carrying this M-60 lighter."

Spike took out his bowie knife and filleted an ear from

matted, bloody hair.

"Don't you ever get tired of that shit?"

"You have a problem?"

"Yeah, I have a problem"

"That's some sick shit," Devil added.

"It ain't like they're fuckin human!" Spike said and spit a hunk of chewing tobacco in the elephant grass. "I mean look at this fuckin ear." He held the spattered ear up to the light like he was examining a dried fig. "That's a fuckin gook's ear!"

"So?"

"So, it ain't fuckin human!"

"You seen what they do to us, Radio," Baby San answered.

"What do they do to us?" asked an FNG.

"For you, sweet lips, something special, something just for Georgia peaches." Devil laughed. "Peach cobbler with nuts!"

"They cut off your dick and balls and stick them in your mouth" Spike said as he poked a small hole through the ear to string it around his neck.

"That's a fucking myth, man. You've never actually seen it."

"I seen it. I seen it in the Ho Bo. Charlie Company."

"That's shit and you know it."

Spike untied his leather necklace and threaded the end through the ear. "Fine, a real fine specimen."

"You're a sick fuck."

"What the fuck you know, Radio. You weren't there. You were still dickin your wife in the World when that shit went down. Charlie was so deep in it, they called in jets, man, jets on their own position. It was a fuckin massacre. We was pullin body parts out of the rubber trees for days. Arms, legs, half a head. Pieces, man. Pieces. Stuck dog tags on the pieces and bagged them up. And some of the heads had dicks and balls stuffed in the mouths. So don't tell me what's right, man. You weren't there." Spike knotted the leather necklace and pulled it over his head.

"They really did that?" asked the FNG.

"Did what?" ripped Lee. "Shit? Everybody does shit. In this fuckin hellhole, everybody does shit."

"What the fuck they teach you at Fort Dix, Peaches? chided Devil. "How to dissemble your gun?" gesturing to his groin.

"How to shoot, I guess."

"Shoot what?" snapped Spike.

"Targets. Enemy soldiers."

"Cardboard, man. Fuckin cardboard men. They didn't train you how to shoot no gook. See this." Spike pulled his necklace off and stuck the string of ears in the FNG's face. "This ain't cardboard, man. This is gook flesh. It belonged to that dead gook over there. Now it belongs to me. I own it. That's all you gotta know. You understand? That's all you gotta know to survive."

"Still ain't right." I said.

Spike pulled the necklace back over his head and leveled his dark blue eyes on me. Sun sparks shot off the blade of his bowie knife as he slowly pointed it toward me.

"Don't you fuckin tell me what's right! You don't know shit 'cept what you hear on that radio, and that ain't real. What's real is this string of ears. Nine, nine mothafuckin gooks that I own for now and for ever. Now you keep talking shit and you'll find yours added to my collection. You got it. We ain't in the "Right" business. We're in the killing business.

Lee stood up.

"Break time's over. Let's move. We ain't got time for this bullshit."

"I got all the respect I need right here." Spike lock and

loaded his M-60 machinegun and panned it across the horizon. He again stopped on the water buffalo grazing about a hundred meters away.

"Impressive, ain't it?" Lonny posed.

"What?" asked Lee.

"Seeing what 20 82's fired for effect can do."

I carried one indelible memory of home with me in the bush, a photo of Janice at Monterey Beach, the last photo I took before leaving for Vietnam.

I'd received a three-day pass after twelve weeks of boot camp and Advanced Infantry Training at Fort Ord.

The first night Janice came up we ate pizza in bed at the Seaside Motel and made love watching old movies. The next morning we'd gone down to Cannery Row.

I'd read about Cannery Row in John Steinbeck's novel my first semester in college at Los Angeles Community College. I was working at Pacific Telephone driving a mail truck and took a full load of classes at night. I thought I'd be reclassified and get a student deferment, but the Draft Board didn't see it that way. I was from the poorest part of the district where the board chose almost all of their quota—they rarely chose boys from their own more affluent neighborhoods—one of the inequities of the Draft Board system that no one talked about--and they'd denied my request for a deferment on a technicality. I'd taken 13 units my first semester, which they considered part-time and 15 units in Winter semester which made me a full-time student for the year. Like many of the ironies of the war, my appeal for a 2S student deferment was approved after I was already drafted and in Vietnam.

Janice and I explored the old fisheries then went back to the motel and made love. We spent more time in bed that weekend then we had for the past year.

Maybe it was Fort Ord, the inevitability of war, the uncertainty and fear that this was the last time we'd ever be together like this again.

Maybe it was the rifle range and the M-16s firing in the distance from night training exercises that punctuated our lovemaking that first Saturday night at the motel.

But as the foghorns blared into the night, again and again I would search for Janice's lips. I found erogenous zones on her body I never even knew existed and kissed her with all the pent-up rage and fear twelve weeks of combat training burned inside me.

She'd worn her salmon-colored sweater and white pants, her light, strawberry-blond hair cut page-boy style, her blue, blue eyes gazing back with a question, her girlish face reflecting ambiguity.

Her cheeks were flush from making love, almost russet, her long legs in white pants teasing the dimple between her thighs.

We'd made love desperately that morning, hungrily, as if we could eat our fears by devouring our bodies, as if I could find another life in the suckling of her breasts, or could fall into her body, disappear inside her clasping pussy and trembling thighs and escape from Vietnam, vanish from the war before I'd even gone.

We bit, sucked, and nipped lips, ears, necks, and breasts, kissed bellies, pubes, pussy, cock and ass, chewed on fingers and eyes and toes and tongues, feasted on our young bodies, our love, our unquenchable fear.

Later, when we walked along the Monterey shore, we took off our shoes and let the waves and white sand wash over our feet, erasing our footsteps as we walked. I asked her to stop, to pause a moment while I snapped a photo.

"What are you thinking?"

"Nothing much."

I dug my hand in the sand, tossed the grains into the wind.

"Come on."

"About time."

"You don't trust me."

"I trust you."

"What then."

"A lot can happen in a year."

"I'll still be here."

"Will you?"

"I love you."

I stood up and walked to where the waves ran up to the edge of the sand. I let the saltwater swirl around my shoes and back out to sea. The cold water drenched my socks and washed over my toes. I picked up some stones and skimmed them off the surface.

Janice came up behind and put her arms around me, whispered in my ear.

"I luvvv you."

I pulled her around and kissed her, a long, slow kiss with my hips pressed tight against hers. I wanted the kiss to last the year I would be gone. I wanted the taste and smell of her to stay with me until I returned.

When I broke the kiss, I whispered I wanted to make love to her.

"Here?"

"No. I don't know. I have to be back in a few hours."

"Is there a place we can go?"

I thought about it a moment as we walked back toward the car. My feet were cold and sloshed in my tennis shoes. Gobs of sand stuck to my socks as I trudged up the dunes and onto the roadway.

We drove up to Fort Ord and out to the firing ranges. As it was Sunday, no one was around. I parked on the side of the road where black cardboard silhouettes of men popped up from the ground.

I climbed into the back seat and tugged on Janice's hand.

"Come on."

She looked like one of my fellow Advanced Infantry trainees low-crawling over a berm as she wriggled over the seat.

"You sure no one will see us?"

"No one comes to the shooting range on Sundays."

I laid out an olive drab wool blanket I'd borrowed from my bed for our beach picnic and pulled it over us a few hundred meters from the rifle range where three days ago I'd put sky-holes in cardboard men.

There was still three weeks before I would graduate from Advanced Infantry Training and a two-week leave before I'd be on my way to Vietnam, but that afternoon I felt this was the last time I'd ever see Janice again.

This afternoon was my goodbye. I would never kiss her with such passion and abandon. She would never see me as the boy she once loved. When we would see each other again, I would be a soldier on the way to a war and she would be a wife-in-waiting.

I would be preoccupied with Vietnam, with combat and the after effects I'd seen in my father, reading the year ahead like tea leaves or a lifeline on a palm.

I'd be shuffling the deck and dealing a hand of black Aces and black Eights.

I'd be weighing my life against the lives of others I'd seen returning from the war.

I made love to Janice in the back seat of my car until my

body was done with love, until I lay against her breast and fell asleep and dreamed her body and mine melting into one another like water or wax or clay. When I awoke the sky sifted from turquoise to salmon to maroon.

I turned the ignition on and drove down the winding road back toward my barracks.

For a long while, neither of us spoke.

What was she doing this moment I wondered?

Was she on her way to school?

Was she at home in our apartment reading a book or watching television.

Was she watching the news of Vietnam?

10,000 miles away, but oh, so much farther in my mind.

No, the distance must be calculated in images and emotions, in blood trails and body counts, in firefights, u-shaped ambushes, and hot LZ's, in wanting kisses and unwritten letters home.

Before I got wounded the first time, I would take out Janice's photo almost every day.

Somehow, by simply gazing at her image, she would be there with me, there like I'd seen her yesterday, or the day before, like she'd just now walked into my bunker or the foxhole where I lay, and was lying there beside me.

Whenever red and green flares parachuted down from the sky from a distant battle, or I sat on a rice paddy dike the morning after a nightlong firefight, or stirred spaghetti C's over heat tabs in the afternoon, I would see her, and would fall in love with her memory once again.

I would imagine her on the beach in Monterey in a salmon-colored sweater and white pants, her cheeks flushed from our morning of making love, the sea breeze tossing a strand of her strawberry blond hair across her blue, blue eyes.

I would see her as we were, so young and so naive, her and I and that still afternoon so long, long ago.

And sometimes when I gazed at her, I wouldn't see the crossed-out days, or this face I live in now.

I would see her, and that moment and the ones after, Tabu sweetening her neck as I leaned close, a sad smile moving across her face.

Even now, if I turn my head just so, I can hear the rat-tat-tat of the M-16s from the rifle range at Fort Ord.

Even now, I can return to her.

These are the moments that I hold as I write these words tonight, as I read this page tomorrow.

There is no time, no memory, no past.

Not now. Not yesterday. Not tomorrow.

There are only these lived moments we imagine again, only this present moment, this door revolving back and forth across time--one turn to enter the past, another to enter now and tomorrow.

Life rushing forward.

Life slowing down.

Life moving at the speed of light, in relative time, flashing through dark matter and waves, these flashbacks real as when I first lived them, these instants slowed by the movement and journey through Time.

I imagine her in a salmon-colored sweater and white pants standing on a sand dune in Monterey.

I look in the mirror--turn one way and see this face--turn another, and see a boy, a young soldier, Janice and her blue, blue eyes.

In Shadow

"Dragon 2/12, this is Charlie 2/12. We've got heavy fire from 360. I repeat we've got heavy fire from 360. Have W.I.A.'s, K.I.A.'s. Request One Cobra. I repeat request One Cobra. That's affirmative. Yes. Yes!"

I heard Charlie Company's firefight on the radio. The Company Commander was dead, and the 2ndplatoon's First Lieutenant shot in the belly. A third of the company was dead, wounded, or missing, and they were on the ragged edge of being overrun. One platoon leader wanted to call in air strikes on themselves. Two Phantoms came and dropped a wall of napalm between them and the charging NVA.

The crackle of flames punctuated the static squelches on my radio.

No one knew the size of the attacking force. Intel said it could be an NVA battalion. That meant Charlie company would be out-numbered eight or ten to one. Since it was late in the afternoon, no other companies could get there to reinforce them that day. There was nothing they could do but set up a perimeter, dig in, and try to hold out for the night.

Mike, came over to Lee and Baby San and me a while later, and told us to saddle up, we were taking our Viet Cong captured mortar into battle. He said he'd volunteered our four-man sixty-millimeter mortar team to lend support for Charlie Company. We got our gear and ammo together and headed out to the landing zone.

Half an hour later, a special chopper came. We loaded our

boxes of 60-millimeter mortar rounds along with my radio, and were whirled up into the night sky.

No infantry company carried 60 millimeter mortars in the bush. They were too heavy, too unwieldy, a discarded weapon from an earlier war.

But when our platoon found a 60 mortar and over five hundred mortar rounds in a cache, Mike wanted to add it to our weapons cache. We already carried a ninety millimeter recoilless rifle, two M-60 machine guns, and numerous L.A.W.s (Light Artillery Weapons), and we were experts with the 81 millimeter mortars at the firebase, so why not add a 60 millimeter mortar to our repertoire?

Before the month was over, we'd honed our mortar-killing-skills through a number of fire fights in the open ground of rice paddies and chaparrals of Tay Ninh province, and achieved a kind of notoriety reserved for LRRP teams (Long Range Reconnaissance Patrols) and madmen.

We humped thirty or forty rounds with us on patrols, each of us carrying an extra ten pounds on backpacks already too heavy to lift onto our backs alone, and became Bravo Company's ace in the hole during firefights and ambushes.

We knocked out mortar and rocket grenade positions 1000 meters away, destroyed dug-in machine guns or command bunkers with a few well-placed rounds, reached farther and were deadlier than any rifle, L.A.W., or grenade launcher that a normal grunt company carried. As our reputation grew, so did the firepower directed against us. A price tag got placed on our heads. In every new firefight, we were the primary target the enemy wanted to kill.

The night was black with a slivered moon, and as the dim flicker of flashlights from the fire support base disappeared beneath us, I felt like I was crossing a dark sea.

Through the open door of the chopper, I could see distant firefights flashing on the ground, and where the horizon bled off into a dark abyss, the blaze of explosions from B-52's carpet-bombing the Ho Bo Woods.

Charlie Company's perimeter wasn't more than a few thousand meters from Pershing. Set up hastily, while under attack and taking heavy casualties, it was more a ragged rectangle bordering two rice paddies than a circular field of fire.

We were dropped inside at around 2200 hours, late, but the makeshift bivouac was still a hive of activity. Guys were feverishly digging in, scooping out moist earth with entrenching tools, filling sandbags two or three high to lay their rifle barrels on, and to duck beneath to save their steel-helmeted heads.

Their foxholes weren't much. Just enough to lay a body down a few inches below the rice paddy dike and maybe save them from flying shrapnel; just enough to lay out twenty or thirty M-16 magazines and six or eight grenades.

Mike found a spot somewhere near the middle of the perimeter and we started digging out a pit large enough for the four of us to lie in and to store our ammo. We set up the mortar in the center of the pit and Mike sighted in on a silhouette of banyan trees about three hundred meters out.

A little past midnight now, and we were ready. Best to get some rest, Mike said, the attack wouldn't come for three or four hours.

He set us up on two-hour guards. Lee would take the first, I the second, Baby San, the third.

On nights like this though, in the lull between a day's firefight and a predawn attack, no one really slept. Adrenaline still raged through our bodies, strumming the tightened cords of our nerves and tendons like a Jimmy Hendrix guitar solo. I dozed between intermittent radio squelches and the rumble of B-52 bombs.

I'd pulled my guard and was awake an hour into Baby San's when a voice cut through the radio's static. One of the listening posts—two-man teams positioned about a hundred meters outside the perimeter on all four sides, the antennae of the main body of the company—called in with movement all around them. Within seconds, another listening post on the opposite side of the perimeter also saw shadows moving through their Starlight Scope's sights and requested to blow their claymore mines and come in.

The company commander was a first lieutenant who'd been in country less than a month. After the firefight earlier that day, when the C.O. and another first lieutenant were wounded, he became the ranking officer and assumed command. He ordered the listening posts to hold off blowing their ambush till they knew how many enemy were there, whether one company was attacking or a full battalion or what.

I'm sure it made perfect sense in Officer's Training School, but out here in the bush, it was suicide, and the men he was ordering knew it.

If they waited too long there would be gooks crawling all around them and they might be caught in a cross-fire between our perimeter and the attacking Vietnamese.

No, they wouldn't wait.

Not tonight, nor tomorrow.

Not for a newbee who knew jack shit about bush-survival, nor for any other officer whose bad judgment or gung ho attitude might cost them the end of their short time.

No, they would wait until the shadows were no longer

shadows and then they would blow their claymore mines, fire their M-16s, heave their six grenades, let loose in a mad minute all the fire power two lightly-armed men could offer, then run like hell back toward the perimeter hoping no friendly would shoot them in the dark, praying to Elephant or Saint Christopher or the God of Charmed Ears they would make it back alive.

By now even guys dug in on the perimeter were seeing green shadows and bushes of elephant grass slowly moving toward them.

Then one of the shadows hit a trip-wire.

A green flare shot up into the pitch black sky and lit the field of fire in front of one of the listening posts.

There were hundreds of dark bodies hugging the ground in front of us like giant lizards pretending to be dead.

Almost simultaneously, the four listening posts blew their claymore mines and started running toward the perimeter.

I don't know if any made it back.

Flares parachuted down from all sides of the perimeter and the rice paddies ignited with explosions and tracers arcing over the dikes.

Mortars walked their way around the shallow foxholes and rocket grenades blasted sandbags into clouds of dust.

M-16's and AK's talked to each other in staccato bursts of rat-rat-rat-tat-tat.

"Mama. Ma…ma. Oh. Oh. Ohhh."

"Medic! Medic!! Medic!!!"

Mike sighted in on an R.P.G. position out about three hundred meters and Baby San fired off five rounds for effect.

My job was to break charges off the rounds and hand them to Lee. Lee then handed them to Baby San who slid them into the mortar tube where they would rocket up into the sky with tails of flame shooting out the tube like tiny comets.

Each charge was a small pouch of gun powder about the size and shape of a long finger attached just below the mortar's fin. The amount of charges determined the range. One charge made the mortar fly about one hundred meters, six charges about six hundred.

Mike sighted in on the target, called the range and direction, Baby San adjusted the mortar accordingly, and I broke the appropriate charges off the rounds. For the R.P.G., I broke off six, leaving four.

"Poomf! Poomf! Poomf! Poomf! Poomf!"

We waited, counted the rounds' trajectories in our heads. In the dark distance, the first round flashed.

Then the second.

Then the third.

Then all.

We waited.

Nothing.

"Five more!" barked Mike.

"Poomf! Poomf! Poomf! Poomf! Poomf!"

Five more rounds lit up the black horizon.

We waited.

Nothing.

Nothing.

The enemy R.P.G. was silent.

Mike sighted in on an enemy mortar about five hundred meters away.

I broke off five charges.

Baby San slid them one by one into the mortar tube.

"To the left. Two." Mike snapped.

Baby San adjusted the tube two clicks to the left and we fired five more.

We waited.

One thousand one. One thousand two. One thousand three. One thousand four. One thousand--

--A flash first. A burst of fire. One. Two. Three. Four. Five. Then the sound of muffled explosions.

"Poomf! Poomf! Poomf! Poomf! Poomf!"

We waited.

If we'd missed, if we were off in our calculations, they would fire back, immediately, ten rounds or more in rapid succession, as answer.

If we were close, close enough for the clay to fly up and fall upon them like hail, or the jagged bits of shrapnel to graze their skin, they would be silent.

By now though, we had become our own bad target.

Between the four M-60 machine guns, the communications bunker, and our mortar, it seemed like we were the odds on favorite for the enemy to kill. Our trail of flame after each mortar round made us an easy target to sight in on.Enemy mortars and R.P.G's came at us from all directions. R.P.G's tore over our heads and exploded in a blaze of fire and thunder on the foxholes around the perimeter directly in front and behind us. Mortars came crashing out of the sky and blasted sandbags, M-16 magazines, and men. They walked all around us with heavy, booming steps.

Terror choked my breath, rushed through my veins like a triple-shot of adrenalin. I felt for the cool fins and bodies of the 60 millimeter rounds, and tuned out everything but tearing off the charges and handing the rounds to Lee.

"Five more." yelled Mike.

We got to three before an R.P.G. ripped through the sandbags surrounding our pit. I was reaching up to grab more rounds when the rocket grenade hit and got knocked backwards into the mud by the blast. A warm liquid streamed down my head and over my face. My ear burned and the side of my head ached like someone had hit it with a lead pipe.

"Ohhh. Fuck!"

Lee crawled over to me and switched on his red-lensed flashlight.

Blood blinded me, spilled down from a deep gash on the left side of my head and coagulated over my eyes like a thin red membrane.

I lay on my back. Red and green tracers streamed by a few inches above me and shot across the night sky.

I couldn't see them anymore, but I could feel their closeness. They smashed into the sandbags around our pit and ticked sand onto my chest and face.

"You're alright, Radio," Lee said as he waved the red-lensed flashlight across my bloody face. "You're gonna be alright."

I didn't believe him.

I didn't believe any of us were going to be alright.

Not that night. Not while mortar rounds exploded a few meters away and I could hear screams through the blasts.

Not while the left side of my head throbbed, blood streamed down, and the blood thickened to a red skin over my eyes.

Lee could see blood spilling down my face, but he couldn't see the wound. He couldn't tell how bad it was--head wounds are bleeders—but what he could see was blood pouring from my head.

I didn't know how badly I was wounded. The side of my head burned like a hundred wasps stung my skull and ear.

But none of that mattered. Not then.

The firefight was raging. I was one among many casualties. Guys were yelling for medics and we were on the verge of being overrun. If that happened, my head wound would become irrelevant.

Mortar rounds exploded all around us.

Hot, heavy hail stones of metal and dirt rained down. Any second we'd be dead.

"Fuck it." I said, "I'm alright."

"Fire!" Mike screamed. "Keep firing! Keep firing!"

"No," the voice in my throbbing head protested. Maybe if we stopped firing, they'd think we were wasted and move on to another target.

The rounds were hitting so close mud and debris rained down every few seconds or so. Ten or twelve rounds walked toward us, exploded around us, and then went past.

Two or three feet closer and they would have hit inside our ten-foot round sandbag pit and killed us all. The next burst of mortars they walked toward us would be our last. I was certain of it and I know Lee and Baby San were thinking that as well.

It was just a matter of time.

But Mike, six months into his second tour, wouldn't have it.

For him, the war was personal. Them, or us. Kill, or be killed. One mortar team against the other. Survival of the strongest will.

So we fired back--one round after another, as fast as Baby San could push them down the throat of the tube.

I didn't think about my wound. I didn't think about wiping the blood off my eyes so I could see. I didn't think about anything but breaking down rounds, firing back, making the eyes and hands on the other side of the explosions think they were off target. If they were on target, we would've laid low, stopped firing, been too afraid to raise our bodies up to fire—at least that's what Mike wanted them to believe.

So I broke down charges as I did before the RPG hit. We

were all dead anyway if the enemy mortar gunner didn't think he was wrong.

We must have fired twenty-plus rounds back before Mike had us pause.

The mortars stopped raining down.

Nothing. Not a single round.

And after awhile, the firefight began to ebb.

An hour later, as dawn broke through the gauze of mist like an orange flare, the field in front of us was silent. Medevacs started swooping down to take out our dead and wounded.

A medic came over, bandaged my head, and walked me to the landing zone.

Half-blind, blood-coagulated gauze circling my head, I thought I'd danced enough with terror that night.

But when the medevac rose about a hundred feet in the air to clear a stand of rubber trees, we suddenly took fire.

Out the open door tipping toward the ground, I saw the flash of AK's firing and heard the rounds shooting up through the thin membrane of the chopper's fuselage and cockpit. The pilot slumped down, and we started to heave and tremble back toward the ground, toward the rice paddies, the North Vietnamese Army, and what I knew was certain death.

Then, with an abrupt lurch, the co-pilot took over. We rose, got more and more altitude, and the muzzle flashes receded into mist. We flew on to Chu Chi and the hospital.

When we touched down on the landing zone, the medic put his arm around my shoulder and helped me out of the med evac. I ducked under the rotor blades and walked through the open doorway where groans, bodies, and a frenzy of doctors and nurses awaited me.

After X-rays, twenty stitches, bottles of Darvon for pain and antibiotics for infection, I was discharged, rehabbed to the

25th Infantry Division's Headquarters at Chu Chi.

I lay my head on the pillow in the Quonset hut at headquarters and thought about Janice, and my mom, and my friends back home.

Now and then, 155 millimeter rounds boomed from the four artillery batteries as grunts called in for support. Phantoms streaked back and forth across the sky carrying their bombs or returning from a sortie. From miles away, the distant explosions of a battle drifted through the hut's thin, aluminum shell.

I no longer believed I'd live forever.

Not with a bloody gauze bandage around my head.

No, luck, luck was all anyone could count on.

Luck saved me when I reached to hand Lee a round and slightly turned my head. I'd turned just enough, one quarter of an inch maybe, so the metal fragments grazed my skull instead of piercing my eye.

Luck saved us when we fired and fired knocking out the enemy mortar before they pumped out more rounds and killed us.

Luck saved our medevac pilot when the bullet lodged in his forehead above his eye instead of inside his brain.

Luck saved us as the co-pilot escaped uninjured and took over the controls before we catapulted into a deadly spin.

Luck.

Not fate.

Not god.

I gazed up at the ribbed metal ceiling of the Quonset hut and composed a letter to Janice in my mind:

Dear Janice,

I'm sorry. I didn't want them to send you a telegram.

I'm okay.

It was nothing really, just a small cut above my ear.

I won't be going back to the field for a few weeks.

I miss you. I wish I were there.

Don't worry.

I'm fine. Really.

I'll write again soon.

I luv you.

I compose the letter, but I don't write it down.

I don't write any letters down while I'm at Division Headquarters.

I wait until I'm back in the bush and receive another letter from Janice.

I answer her questions, say everything is fine, say don't worry, don't worry, don't worry. I'm fine, I'm fine, I'm really fine.

I volunteered to go back to the bush early. I got tired of thinking about home.

There were no helicopters headed to Pershing so they put me on a convoy with FNG's, rehabbed casualties, and slackers.

I hated convoys. Shit always happened on convoys. Booby traps, mines, snipers, ambushes—something always happened driving along Highway 1 from Chu Chi to Trang Bang.

The deuce-and-a-halfs were slow, cumbersome, open-bedded trucks. They plodded along with twenty plus soldiers loaded in the back, bumping up and down over potholes, and hanging on to the railing.

When the convoy slowed, eight or ten kids would run alongside begging for cokes and candy bars.

"G.I. numba 1! G.I. numba 1! You gimme coca cola, eh, G.I.?!"

And some FNG would toss a coke or a candy bar or a C-rat.

When I tossed a Baby Ruth, the guy sitting next to me

started jabbering.

He was black, 25 maybe, a half-smile working across his face.

"They ain't your fucking friend, man. None of these mothafuckas be your friend. They be the enemy sure as rain. Eight year old boys and boom boom girls. Be spying on you to tell the Viet Cong. Next thing you know you be blown up by C-4 in a coke can. You think I'm jiving? I ain't jiving. Blew up my buddy "Red" with a Doctor Pepper filled with nails and shit. Couldn't recognize his black face with all the holes. Looked like craters on the dark side of the moon 'cept they was blood-red. Now me, I don't give no gook kid no coca cola. I give 'em what they deserve."

He unclips a grenade from his ammo belt and stands up.

"Here you go gook mothafucka!" He makes a slow, sweeping motion with his arm and under-hands the grenade into the crowd of kids. At the last moment, he slows his arm, and the grenade jumps about a foot up in the air. He catches it as the truck hits a pothole and bucks everyone off the bench. The kids scatter like pigeons. The soldiers sitting next to him move away. Even with the pin still in, it's crazy dangerous, and no one wants to be around him.

I scoot away, keep my distance, as the kids start chanting "G.I. numba 10! G. I. numba 10!" One of the bravest flips him the finger.

He laughs and sits back down, grabs my arm to pull me closer. I can see the red-glared eyes of gonza weed. He's high as a kite.

"You coulda milked that wound for another month in Chu Chi, if you wanted." He was looking at the gauze bandage on the side of my head.

"You, gung ho? A fuckin lifer?—"

"No, I just—"

"--Me, I been dodging bullets since I got here. Been in the boonies, been in the shit. But the shit ain't no place for a black man like me. To easy to get my black ass killt. They put me on point. They put me on night patrol, L.P.'s, you name it. They want me to go down in some gook spider hole. But I ain't no tunnel rat. I ain't going down in no hole. No way. No how.

"I ain't doing it, I tells 'em. I ain't getting kilt for no white man's war. 'Ain't no business for a black man to be fightin a yellow man in the Vietnam.' That's what my man Muhammad Ali say, so that's what I tells 'em.

"But they don't hear me. They sends me out on a suicide mission. Eight of us. Six black and two brown. Like we was disposable, another body to count. To search an' destroy a fuckin ville where nobody live. A ghost town. Even the water buffalo and chickens done left. The VC was waitin for us. They knew we was coming. They always know. Can smell us a mile away. Had a U-shaped ambush waiting. AK's and RPG's comin at us from all directions. Cut us up like watermelon on the 4thof July."

The convoy stops, waits for the combat engineers to check out the road for mines.

He gets agitated by the delay, leaps up and goes into his fake grenade-throwing bit again.

"Hey, you gook mothafuckas, you want a co-ca co-la?"

There aren't any takers. The kids have scattered and aren't coming back. No one wants to get close to the crazy man.

I hop off the truck.

My head hurts. Sweat saturates the gauze bandage and stings the raw flesh.

I don't want to be here. I don't want to get back on the truck. I wander up the line of trucks and hop on another one.

A medic took my stitches out at Pershing.

I rubbed the rough scab off the scar and slipped the steel pot over my head slowly, sweat burning the raw, pink flesh.

Then I slid the PRC-25 radio straps over my shoulder and headed out on a search and destroy mission.

When I returned to the base camp that night, Mike said tomorrow there would be a ceremony to honor the dead and wounded from Charlie Company. I needed to be there so the battalion commander could pin a Bronze Star and Purple Heart onto my jungle fatigues, shake my hand, and award me for my courage under fire.

Tomorrow.

Tomorrow, I would salute the others, honor posthumously Charlie Company's four dead, pay my respects to the Captain and the First Lieutenant and the fifteen other soldiers killed or wounded in action.

Tomorrow, I would wonder again, what I did to receive a Bronze Star with a V for Valor under fire.

Tomorrow, I would ask myself again, what courage has to do with terror.

I could've laid there and waited for the medic to come.

I could've let the blood pouring down my face consume me with fear and not fired back.

Maybe Mike, Lee and Baby San would've survived the battle without me.

Maybe.

Maybe not.

Maybe the enemy mortar team would've realized we were hit and fired ten more rounds for effect and we would all be dead.

"Keep firing!" Mike said. "Keep firing!"

And so I did, despite my fear, despite my pain, despite being blinded by blood pouring over my eyes.

I broke down charges and handed the rounds to Lee, and Baby San loaded them in the tube, and we kept firing, desperately, frantically, as if the rounds landing all around us weren't close, as if we were all immortal, as if none of us would ever die.

For Mike, that was courage under fire: A small sacrifice by one that probably saved us all.

I never quite understood it. Not then.

Not until many, many years later, when I stood in front of The Wall and grieved.

Even then, it wasn't my courage I remembered, but my honor—my honor for the men beside me, and my honor for those who didn't survive.

After the ceremony, I unpinned my Bronze Star and Purple Heart, and put them in a plastic bag with the rest of my souvenirs—my NVA uniform patch, my strand of trip wire from the dud round I triggered my first week in the field, a blood-spattered Ace of Spades.

I took off my clean, green fatigues, and slipped back inside my old clothes.

I smelled the blood and mud and sweat and was flooded with a rage I still possess.

Then I headed out on patrol, listened to the distant voices on the radio, and vowed again never to die here, to place another X on hell's calendar--sixty-three days now and tomorrow the sixty-fourth.

I didn't feel like a hero.

Heroes are unknown soldiers, ghosts who live in the subterranean home of the brave.

Heroes are the "Smiles" of the world.

Not survivors.

Not I.

We reached our night laager position as the light rolled toward dusk and began to dig shallow foxholes.

After about 20 minutes, Mike came back from headquarters. He was deadpan.

"C. O. wants an L.P."

"From us? But we're the weapon's platoon." spat Devil.

"We're already shorthanded," protested Lee.

"Not as short-handed as the rest of the platoons, I guess. We've got 20, the others, less than 16."

"How're we gonna man the mortars?" asked Baby San.

"We'll use three man teams tonight, be one short. Lee will man the radio. Here."

Mike handed me the L.P. radio.

"You and Lonny. You're it for tonight."

"I thought we were done with L.P.s."

L.P.s were for FNGs like stirring the company's shit in fifty gallon drums at Firebase Pershing, not for guys with three months in the bush.

But there weren't any new guys, not since the last two got blown up from a mine on Highway 1 heading back from Trang Bang.

"Last in, first out. Always the same shit." grumbled Lonny.

"Where?" I asked.

"Here's the map and the checkpoint. 9 o'clock, 300 meters out."

"300 meters? You gotta be fuckin kidding! That's NVA bait, man."

"How the fuck you expect us to get back from there?" Lonny protested.

"On wings, man. On fucking angel's wings and a prayer," Baby San laughed sarcastically.

"On fuckin Devil's wings," shot Lonny. "This is hell, remember?"

"No, man. Hell's just got fire and brimstone, not AK's and RPGs. The bush is worse than Hell, right Spike?" added Baby San.

Spike looked up from wiping mud off his M-60. "I don't know what Hell looks like. I ain't never been there, and I ain't never going."

"Yeah, I remember, God's on your side." spat Devil.

"Look, I don't like this shit anymore than you do." Mike jumped in. "But the old man's worried. Says intelligence believes there's an NVA Brigade out there. He's putting out three L.P.s. One from first platoon, one from third, and one from us."

"So we're the fucking bait for an NVA Brigade? Are you fucking serious?" Lonny snarled.

"Intel always comes up with this shit. It's never true." I said.

But I knew even intel's fuck-ups led to bad judgment calls. We were always put in dangerous situations due to shitty intel. That was Smile's story. That's why they had to call jets in on themselves.

"No wonder the old man's worried. If intel's right, Bravo company's the bait. Me and you, we're just the chum."

"What the fuck's 'chum'?"

"It's the bloody shit you throw in the water to attract bigger fish to the real bait."

"The real bait?"

"The bait on a hook."

"Great. So we're the chum for an NVA Brigade."

"Stop fucking complaining. Neither of you have been on L.P.'s or night patrol for over a month because we had new guys. Well, we don't have any new guys right now so you're gonna have to be the new guys for a while. Spike and Devil, you're up next."

"The poor man's Army in action. Equal opportunity for all, "I jibed.

"Yeah, everyone gets the opportunity to get equally dead." Devil snapped.

"When?" I asked.

"Now. The C.O. wanted you in place by 1800."

"That was over a half hour ago."

"Yeah. We're late getting here, late getting intel, and late digging in. And we've still got another two hours getting the pit ready. Saddle up, Radio. And make sure you take some extra grenades, smoke, and flares." ordered Mike.

"Flares?"

"For backup."

"Backup for what?" Lonny asked, suspicious of what Mike meant.

"In case we get pinned down and they need to see us." I answered.

I knew there was more to it than that. The flares were in case we had to call in jets or artillery on our own position, in case they needed to see us if we were overrun.

We packed up our shit and got ready to leave the perimeter.

I stuffed two flares, two claymores, four grenades, three smoke canisters, and thirty M-16 magazines into my backpack. Lonny packed the same, then added two more flares, 'just in case.'

We were ready for a war--just not a very long war. A five minute war maybe, and then we'd be out of ammo, di-di-maoing back to the perimeter, hoping our soldiers wouldn't fire at us as we ran toward them through the dark.

We were the last L.P. to leave.

No one paid much attention.

Everyone was busy, getting ready for a night attack, digging foxholes, building up berms to lay their rifles on, laying out their field of fires.

We stopped at the line of the perimeter and looked at the two guys whose foxhole was a straight line to our L.P.

"If you fucking shoot me when I'm di-di-maoing back, my ghost will come back and waste you motherfuckers." Lonny ripped.

They looked up from their work and gave us a sarcastic smile like "You sorry fuckers. Like ghostsare gonna scare us!"

We moved out of the perimeter and snaked toward the darkening horizon. Ahead, a stand of mangroves looked like giant warriors in the twilight.

I didn't know how far they were. A little over two hundred meters, I guessed.

"There." I whispered to Lonny. "No farther."

"I'm with you, man. Fuck the C.O."

"That's at least two hundred meters."

"Two hundred meters too far."

"Ten meters is too fuckin far if we get hit."

"You sound like a short-timer."

"I am a short-timer."

"Yeah, only 265 days to go."

"264, man. I got a day on you, my brother."

"Aces and Eights, man. Aces and Eights all the way down the line."

Darkness slid over us like skin as we moved farther away from the perimeter. The banyans were black silhouettes now, barely visible against the darker horizon.

We no longer spoke.

Not now.

Not when even a loud whisper could give us away.

So we walked in silence, each step burdened with uncertainty, each swish of our boots slipping through the elephant grass taking us deeper into terror.

Night now, the dark fallen down upon us like a black parachute as we reached the mangroves.

We set up four claymore mines to cover the field of fire in front of us, and strung a small perimeter of tripwires attached to flares about ten feet ahead of the claymores.

If the NVA were walking, camouflaged with brush, heading toward the company perimeter, someone's foot would trip the unseen, monofilament wire, and a flare would shoot up into the sky and light the field of fire like a firework on the fourth of July.

We'd blow the claymores, fire our M-16s, hurl our grenades, and di-di-mao like sprinters back to the company perimeter.

That was the plan anyway.

But the NVA commanders were often smarter than our plan.

With a history of fighting invaders for over a thousand years, the Vietnamese army wasn't about to expose the main body of their soldiers without the element of surprise. Like us, they would send out scouts, chum for the larger firefight to come.

If the scouts triggered a booby-trapped flare, only they would be sacrificed. Night, and the elephant grass, would keep the rest of the brigade from being seen.

And if they were low-crawling, slithering through the tall grass slow as "fuck-you" lizards, snaking toward where they knew we'd bivouacked in, their hands might catch the tripwire before it snapped even if it were strung taut as a violin wire.

Our Starlight Scopes however, could trump their scouts.

Harvesting moon and starlight like rain and amplifying it 50,000 times, we could see their gray-green shadows moving in the dark.

Not clearly. Not as real bodies. More like disembodied spirits--vague, green-tinged figures slipping through the darker shades of brush, grass and trees.

10:33.

I took the first guard.

I panned the Starlight slowly across the field of fire. Every bush moved. Every tuft of grass shifted like a head camouflaged by a crown of elephant grass. And there were many heads, and they were low-crawling toward us.

I pulled the Starlight from my eye, waited till my night vision returned, and panned again.

Nothing.

No one.

The heads gone--or stilled.

I panned from left to right a second time. Slowly.

Still nothing.

Whatever I saw the first time was no longer there.

Starlight phantoms.

If you looked long enough through the Starlight, especially if you starred at one spot, a wave of ghostly bodies often seemed to be moving toward you through the grass.

But if you closed your eyes, and let the dark soak in for thirty seconds, when you looked through the Starlight again, the ghosts would be gone, vanished from the grass.

10:51.

Quiet. So very, very quiet.

Above, a black parachute beaded with a billion glittering

stars. The night sky immense, wondrous. I could make out The Big Dipper pouring a bucketful of suns. I could see The Bear, and The Seven Sisters rising in the dark horizon.

What were we doing here?

We lay in the arms of a mangrove, in a 4' by 6' patch of earth, waiting for an enemy to appear, to rise up out of the elephant grass with their AKs flashing in the vast, unfathomable night.

How insignificant we were under the immense night sky!

If there were other lives beyond us--me, gazing up at these stars, Lonny resting so quiet beside me—they were lost in this limitless dark.

No, there was just us, Lonny and I, one black man and one white man hugging the mangrove's roots like arms; dark, brown arms wrapped around us in the darker night; me gazing through the Starlight and Lonny sleeping--no, not sleeping, dreaming, half-dreaming—and somewhere around us, the enemy reaching toward us like phantom limbs.

11:54.

Almost midnight.

In a few minutes I would wake Lonny, roll under my poncho and try to sleep.

I could barely make out his body under the green blanket.

What was he dreaming of in his half-sleep?

About his girlfriend in Oakland? About his mother who sent him letters every week? About his younger brother who just turned eighteen and was now eligible for the draft?

Somewhere behind us was Devil, Baby San, Mike, Lee, our platoon, our company, the C.O., headquarters, our men--safe, safer than us, safer than this tree, these roots we hug as if a mother's arms, this dark, wet earth we lie upon.

I wish I could disappear inside this ground, be root, tree,

grass, dirt, water, something other than this body, this breath, this heart—heart, my heart beating so loudly against my ribcage anyone crawling toward us could hear--and Lonny dreaming, turning inside his dream, the sky above no longer sky but cosmos, a trillion, trillion stars, so immense I disappear, I dissolve—not into earth, not into root and worm, but into the infinite, domed night, into the twinkling fires of dying stars…

And then I return—to my body, to my drumming heart, to Lonny breathing beside me, to our tiny, desperate lives.

11:56.

How Time slows in the vastness of this night?

A shooting star becomes a life passing—darkness into light, light into darkness again…

I should wake Lonny, sleep.

Two hours and a wakeup and we're halfway home.

But I don't wake him.

I stare into the night sky and imagine Janice on the other side of the World.

What is the hour? The day?

Night slips through my fingers as I count: 14 hours. Behind. Yesterday.

She's returning from school. Changing to go to work--at the grocery store, Lucky's, where I used to work my senior year in high school; where she boxes groceries in the afternoons, places meat and milk and eggs in a paper bag and daydreams about Monterey.

Or she's at home, reading a book, washing dishes, taking a shower.

Or she's dreaming as Lonny's dreams, dreaming of me, of us, here, in this shallow sump, hugging the roots of a banyan like arms.

"Here's looking at you," I used to say—my favorite

"Casablanca" line--sitting at our small, kitchen table, in our one bedroom apartment on Florence Avenue in Bell.

Bell, California.

Ten blocks from the trailer park ghetto where I grew up.

But nice. Nicer. Almost middle class.

Two kids. 19 and 17. In love. Making a home.

What was it like for her to watch the news, to get telegrams that her 19 year old husband was wounded?

He was alive, yes, but in a hospital, recuperating in the base camp. Waiting to go back to the war.

12:13.

Lonny turns in his dream, startles awake, stares at me as if he's awakened from the dead.

He starts to tell me something, something important, something that he saw in his dream.

Then stops. He can't. He knows he can't. Not now. Not here.

He sits up, stares at me, looks at the illuminated digits on his watch: 12:14.

Why didn't I wake him up, he gestures.

I shrug, smile, roll over onto my back, lose myself in the stars fringed by grey-green mangrove branches.

I close my eyes, feel the wetness beneath my skin.

Not cold, but wet. A warm wetness like piss or blood.

Somewhere through the stars is Janice, home, "The World".

I see her cheeks flush from making love, her long legs slung over my thighs, her blue, blue eyes gazing back with a question.

2:11

"Shhh!"

A hand clasps my mouth, muffling sound.

"Movement!" he whispers.

"Where?" I mouth.

He points: 9 o'clock. Pans across the line of fire: 12 o'clock.

I look, can't see anything, put the Starlight to my eye.

To my left, about 100 meters out, the elephant grass shifts in a slight wind. Choppy waves of grey-green grass surge toward us--broken, uneven, ripples of grey-green waves in a blackened sea—but no heads, no faces, no eyes.

I stop, pan the Starlight across, stop dead center from where we lie.

The grass is sparser there, clumps of brush amidst patches of dark green grass. I see heads. No, not heads exactly, but crowns of bushes bobbing in a black sea. How many? 20? 50? I can't count. The whole ground seems to be rolling toward us like an enormous wave.

"Fuck! We gotta di-di-mao man! We gotta blow this shit and di-di to the perimeter. Now!"

"Call it in!"

"I'm on it."

I muffle my voice, but I'm too loud and I know it. I don't give a shit. We need to blow the L.P. and run. It doesn't matter if they hear us now.

"Dragon one, this is Dragon Watchtower. We've got movement at checkpoint alpha. We're red-charging and coming in. Do you read me, Dragon One, we're red-charging and coming in."

"Roger, Dragon watch tower. We copy. Need estimate and direction on movement."

"200. Maybe more. 9 and 12 o'clock from Alpha. 100 meters. Request permission to blow watchtower. I repeat, request permission to blow watchtower!"

"Fuck, man. They're already here. 10 o'clock. Look."

I looked where Lonny was pointing, about 25 meters out.

I could see clumps of bushes slowly moving unevenly toward us over the ground.

"Dragon One we're red-charging and coming in. I repeat. We're red-charging and coming in!"

"Dragon Watch Tower, hold fire. Need to affirm.I repeat. Hold fire. Need to affirm Victor Charlie position."

"No can do. Charlies in henhouse. Coming in."

"Ready Lonman?"

"Ready."

We pushed the plungers down on the claymores and simultaneously fired into the darkness 25 meters out, laying a line of fire about a foot above the ground. Three bursts and our magazines were unloaded. I shoved another magazine in the slot, turned and ran after Lonny racing down the trail.

Bullets and RPG's were already crashing and exploding around us. When one RPG sailed over our heads and hit a foxhole on the perimeter, soldiers on the line opened fire.

Suddenly we were running into fire as well as away. Tracers criss-crossed the trail and came from all directions.

AK-47s, RPGs, and mortars erupted from all sides of the perimeter. The NVA we saw in front of us through the Starlight were actually all around us now.

Bullets and explosions came from every direction. Soldiers on the perimeter were blowing claymore mines and laying fields of fire directly where we were running.

Lonny was zigzagging about 10 meters ahead.

"Lonny! Lonny! Stop!" I screamed trying to catch up to him.

A burst of machine gun fire from the company's perimeter and he was gone.

I tripped over him full stride and sprawled onto the

elephant grass about ten feet away. RPGs and mortars hurled mud and grass on top of me as I lay face down on the ground.

Through the explosions, I could hear moans: Lonny. I low-crawled to the sound and found him crumpled on his side, in a half-fetal position.

"Lonny! Lonny!!! Fuck!"

I scanned the red-lensed flashlight over him but I already knew he was bad. Blood spurted from his neck. A hole large as my fist pulsed near his chest.

His breath was a gurgle, his voice a ragged whisper between unintelligible words.

I rolled him toward me and saw a fearful, dim stare in his eyes. He mouthed something as I moved the flashlight to his neck and found a large gaping hole and blood spurting.

I put my palm over the wound and dug into my pack to find compression bandages and gauze to fill the holes.

"Hold on, Lonny. Hold on. You're going to be alright."

I couldn't stop the bleeding. Not from his neck. Not from his chest. His lungs were collapsing and I knew an artery was severed in his neck. He was losing too much blood, too fast. Within a few minutes, he would choke on his own blood and his heart would stop. I couldn't save him. No one could.

I wrapped my poncho around him, put my arm under his head, and held him.

"It's okay, man. It's okay. Just rest. Just close your eyes and rest."

He mouthed words I couldn't hear.

Didn't matter. I knew what he wanted and would've given it to him if I could. I would've prayed for it, if a prayer could've saved him, though by then, I no longer believed in gods.

Explosions and bullets smashed into the ground where we lay. The smell of burnt flesh charred the air. Flares lit a gray-green field punctuated by intermittent fires.

I pulled the poncho over us and pretended we were dead.

"It's okay, Lonny. It's okay. Just close your eyes. I'm here. I'm...here."

He mumbled something. I wasn't sure what it was—"home...mom...love..."—something.

"It's okay, Lonny....it's...okay."

5:43

Light woke me, sun breaking through the smoke and mist.

And moans.

Not from Lonny. No, he was gone. But from someone else, close, 10 meters maybe.

I uncovered Lonny's face and gazed at him in the dim light.

His skin was grey-white in the dawn, bloodless, the gaping hole in his throat looked like a dark mouth, empty, torn, a black hole swallowing the light. His eyes were still open, starring up at the new sky, the blue, effervescent haze rising from the field, eerie as spirits stirring in a graveyard.

I lay my bloody hands over Lonny's eyes, shut them, and pulled the poncho over his body. Red tears streaked my face.

I lifted my head to see where the company perimeter was.

Smoke, embers, ashes, arms, legs, body parts and torn flesh—smashed AKs, spent bullet cartridges, RPG and mortar fragments, shrapnel, small craters, blackened grass, the stand of mangrove trees where we'd set up for the night splintered and jagged, tree stumps jutting up from the ground like broken legs.

Not far from where we lay, I again heard a groan and a slight rustle like an animal moving through the grass.

I looked out over the berm and saw a body bobbing through the burnt patches. He was moving toward us, but was about ten meters off line. He couldn't see me.

He was wounded, his arms pulled him, but his legs were useless, both were bloody, one was shoeless, frayed, the foot a ragged mess of flesh.

I raised my M-16 to my shoulder and took aim. He must've heard the rattle because he swiveled his head and found me.

His face was streaked with blood and char. He didn't have a weapon. I doubt if he could have pulled a trigger. His hands were just as bloody as his legs, and looked more like claws pulling him along the ground. He starred at me, turned away, and continued crawling.

I got off two rounds ticking the dirt a few meters in front of him. He stopped, turned toward me again, and laid his head down as if waiting for me to shoot him.

One burst and he was done. Gone. Like Lonny. Like me. Like all of us in this killing field.

Kill him! Kill him! He's a gook, not a man!

That was the voice I heard in boot camp and A.I.T. (Advanced Infantry Training), the voice that droned into me like a mantra: **They are gooks, dinks, commies, savages, nothing resembling us, nothing close to human.**

And, it worked--when I was shooting at a cardboard man, when I was stabbing a dummy to death with a bayonet, when I was on the edge of terror--it was the only voice I heard.

But four months in Vietnam changed me.

The kids along Highway 1 chanting "G.I. Numba One" as they begged for a chocolate bars or cokes looked no different than the kids from my tenement—Asian versus black, or Puerto Rican, or Pollock, or Jew—hungrier maybe, more desperation in their eyes. But under the grime and stink, they were no different then the kids I grew up with, each carrying hopes and fears and dreams.

And so I heard another voice—my own. For a few months

anyway.

Then the dead and dying took root inside me and my eyes deadened, became dark and still as the eyes of a corpse.

How long does it take to kill a man--from inside? How many day-after-crossed-off-days does it take for the kills to wash off like blood, till I was no longer shooting human beings, but pigs or chickens or water buffalo. How long before I was no longer a man but a rifle, a bullet, an I inside a soulless body?

The voice said to kill this dying man—for Lonny, for Smiles, for everyone I lost and loved.

"Kill! Kill! Kill!" it commanded.

So I raised my rifle and took aim just below his eyes.

He wasn't afraid. Somewhere during the night, he'd passed through death's door. He was on the other side now, closer to Lonny than to me.

If I were his executioner, so be it.

I put his head in the crosshairs, held my breath, and put my finger on the trigger guard.

I didn't squeeze the trigger.

I couldn't.

Not anymore.

Lonny was dead. Nothing I could do would bring him back.

Not killing this soldier. Not killing the whole fucking North Vietnamese Army.

Lonny was dead.

Shot in the throat and chest by his own men. Friendly fire. Friendly. As if killing was somehow friendlier if done by your own men.

And who was to blame?

The soldiers on the perimeter who opened fire from fear of being overrun?

The C.O. who sent us out?

General Westmoreland? Nixon? Kissinger? The Pentagon? The Army? The rich? The whole fucking US of A? My mother? My war-hero father?

Yes, everyone was to blame. Everyone carried Lonny's blood on their hands.

I lowered my rifle.

I was done.

I was done with killing, done with death, done with war.

For a long moment, the wounded soldier held my eyes, then he turned and slowly crawled away.

6:51

Dawn's mist vanished.

Night's ghosts returned to their shallow graves.

A noxious odor rose from the field as the sun boiled blood and flesh.

I called in.

"Dragon One, this is Watchtower. Hold fire. Returning to henhouse. I repeat, Watchtower returning to henhouse. Hold fire."

"Watchtower, what's your situation?"

I turned the radio back to mute.

I didn't have anything to say.

I wrapped Lonny up in my poncho and slung him over my shoulder. I took a step and fell face down in the grass.

I couldn't carry both Lonny and the radio on my back.

I tied the ends of the poncho in a knot and dragged him toward the perimeter.

It was tiring and slow and I was an easy target, but the company perimeter wasn't far, maybe 50 meters over charred, open ground, besides no one else in the field was still alive.

7:34

I was about 20 meters away when the two soldiers we passed going out spotted me.

They came running out to help and started to grab the poncho.

I leveled my M-16 on them.

"Get the fuck away!" I screamed.

"Hey!. Hey! We're just trying to help you, man."

I don't need your fuckin help!"

I drug Lonny into the perimeter as a crowd of soldiers gathered to watch.

"Fuck, what happened."

"LP, man."

"Bad shit. Last night was some bad shit."

"What's wrong with that guy?"

"Crazed, man. Crazed."

I didn't pay them no mind. I just kept dragging Lonny to our platoon.

Devil saw me first.

"No, man, no! Not Lonny! No, no, no, no, no!"

They were all around us now, pulling Lonny out of the poncho. A medic came over and started looking at his wounds. Lee called headquarters.

Mike slammed his steel pot against the ground.

"Tell headquarters we're firing some H & I's."

"But there's no targets, Mike."

"I'll find some fuckin targets. Tell them I'll call in the grids when I have them."

"C.O. is saying no firing till we have a target."

"Fuck the C.O. Tell him LP confirms a mortar position!"

"But—"

"Just fuckin tell him! Baby San, Devil, start breaking down rounds."

"How many? Where?"

"12 o'clock. 400 meters. 20."

"For effect?"

"No. I want you to walk them. In fives. 10 meters apart. Now!!!"

I dumped the LP radio near Lonny's body and walked off.

I didn't know where I was going.

I was just gone. Long gone.

I didn't know if I'd ever return.

When your best friend dies, you don't suck it up like a man.

You don't swallow his death like a bitter pill and hump on down the trail.

You want to kill someone.

You want to unload your magazine on anyone you can find.

A Viet Cong. A papa san. A mama san. A boom boom girl. A pig. A water buffalo. The Company Commander. Some thing living. Some thing that bleeds.

You want to fire and fire and fire till the rage dies inside you, till the pain bleeds through into someone else.

You want to scream "Burn, baby, burn!" as you run through village after village torching the hootches one by one.

You want to beat the butt end of your M-16 against someone's skull till the hurt inside drowns in their blood.

You want to, but you don't.

You can't.

You need to hold onto the one piece of yourself that's not death, that's not war.

So you don't kill anyone.

Not then anyway.

Later.

Later, you might beat someone to death for no reason.

Later, you might throw a grenade into a hootch and blow away a family of "suspected" Viet Cong.

Later, you might go crazy out of grief and kill innocent civilians—a woman, a child, an old man, someone, anyone.

But today, you'll suck it up, stuff it down, swallow it like a rotten egg.

Today, they'll load a piece of you in the body bag with Lonny and helicopter you back to "The World".

A piece today, and a piece tomorrow, and a piece till your tour is done; a piece and a piece and a piece till every piece of you that is good is gone, body-bagged and tagged for home, till what is left inside is hollow, empty, ready to kill anything that moves, anything that breathes, anything that loves.

In Light

Trang Bang wasn't the same after Lonny's death.

Oh, the faces of the villagers were just as blank and empty.

But I could read something else beyond the blankness now: the same dead stare the dying Vietnamese soldier held in his eyes--an emptiness like stone markers marking unknown graves.

Yet, each face owned a name, and in the eyes there was hate and anger, a hate I rarely saw before.

It was not unlike the hate I witnessed in Watts during the riots in 1966. The silent rage of blacks as they were being handcuffed after being beaten by police. The same silent rage I owned whenever a police car came patrolling down my street looking for criminals.

To the poor whites and Hispanics where I grew up, the police were invaders, ready to violently attack anyone who crossed their path.

I remembered how they'd handcuffed and beaten my high school friends and I one night after a party. I was seventeen at the time, and yes, we were too loud, too amped up with alcohol and male hormones to not have a neighbor complain. When my friend answered the door, six huge Sheriffs Deputies stood outside. They must have been over six foot tall and weighed at least 220 pounds. None of us were over 5'6" and 160 pounds. And we weren't threatening, unless a few stupid, drunk comments were threatening.

But four drunk and loud seventeen and eighteen year old

high school kids didn't mean we should be severely beaten on the way to jail.

Handcuffed and painfully thrown into the back seat of two patrol cars, I wondered why we stopped at a dark, vacant gas station on the way to the jail.

It didn't take long to find out.

The six cops slid tight leather gloves over their hands and took us out one by one and punched us in the stomach and ribs. They were careful not to leave any marks, two of us being under-aged and all. But one hit my buddy Wayne so hard, he broke three ribs, and Wayne spent the next four months with a brace wrapped around him. He couldn't even dance at the prom because his ribs hurt too much to move.

How powerful they must've felt! Six large, muscular men with guns and billy clubs, each outweighing us by almost a hundred pounds, each believing in the lie of power, in bullying someone who is weaker, smaller, powerless to fight back.

As we humped across the Trang Bang Bridge, I remembered how we felt when the police officers towered over us with their guns and billy clubs ready. I watched the Vietnamese civilians sitting cross-legged in front of their hootches, cowering with their empty eyes, and I felt ashamed.

We shouldn't fuckin be here. None of us. We weren't saving anyone. That was all a lie. One more lie to put next to Lonny's death, and every Vietnamese we counted as bodies instead of lives.

"I hate these mothafuckers!" shot Spike as he pointed his M-60 muzzle at a mama san who was at least 80 years old.

"Looks to me like you ain't on their top ten list either," spit Devil.

"We oughta just napalm this fuckin village and be done with it. I'm sure we wouldn't have to worry about no more snipers or mortars."

"Leave her the fuck alone, Spike. She's too old to be firing mortars or RPG's at us."

"How the fuck you know, Radio? These bastards can do a lotta shit. I bet this mothafucker right here's been sniping at us every time we leave from this ville."

Spike pushed the M-60 muzzle up against the mama san's nose. "It was you, wasn't it, mothafucker?"

"Leave her the fuck alone!!!" I shoved Spike away hard and stood between him and the mama san. "Can't you see she's so scared she's trembling!"

"Scared!? I want her to be fuckin scared! She should be fuckin scared 'cause I am one bad motherfucka!" He tried to move around me but I blocked him again. This time he leveled his M-60 on me.

"Listen, you sick motherfucka, if you don't move your M-60 outta my face, I'm gonna waste your fuckin ass!"

"What the hell are you two assholes doing?!" Mike screamed. He moved between Spike and I and pressed his M-16 muzzle against Spike's neck. "You ever point your weapon at anyone in this platoon again, you're gonna have an accident on night patrol, a fatal fuckin accident! Radio, call the C.O. and tell him we've searched and secured our position."

I backed off Spike and radioed the C.O.

"He wants to know if we found anything?"

"Tell him we found the same nothing we've found for the last three months. Tell him—Fuck it, I'll tell him. Gimme the horn! Lee, escort John Wayne here to a safe position. I don't want him starting a war with innocent, old papa sans!"

"Innocent!? Who the fuck do you think is sniping at us?"

Spike wasn't ready to back down. One of his redneck buddies got killed by a sniper a few days ago and he was bent on some measure of revenge.

"Get him the fuck outta here before I have to shoot him for disobeying my commands!"

Lee pushed Spike on down the road as Mike grabbed the horn from me.

"Innocent!!! None of you gook mothafuckers are innocent," he yelled, as Lee pushed him away.

"They're caught in the crossfire, you dumb piece of shit," I yelled back. "What do you expect!"

"Radio, shut the fuck up! I don't need you playing Mother Teresa neither! Get on the horn and tell the C. O. we got nothing here."

"Dragon one, this is Dragon four. We got nothing. I repeat. We've got nothing at checkpoint Alpha. Please advise."

"Roger that! No Victor Charlies. No weapons. Nothing…Okay. Torch a few hootches and proceed to LZ."

"Mike, the CO wants us to burn some hootches before we head out."

"What the fuck for?"

"To make a point, I guess."

"What point? Like Hell needs us to light more fires?"

"This is sick, Mike. This whole fucking war is some sick mothafucka's wet dream!" I snapped.

"Shut up, Radio! Just move the fuck out! Lee, torch 'em, and let's move the fuck out!"

December 26th, 1968, was the last day I owned my name.

We'd returned on Christmas Eve from a month in the Ho Bo Woods.

We'd been ambushed, mortared, rocketed, booby trapped, and sniped at almost every day and were happy to finally be back at the Fire Support Base.

Doc Foster, one week shy of transferring out of the bush, lost half his right hand from a Rocket Propelled Grenade as he ran to help a wounded point. My friend "Florida" from 2ndPlatoon, and two new guys, went out with a squad on night patrol and never came back. A chunk of another new guy's shoulder hit my boot during a sniper attack. I watched a medic stuff a compress over the hole to stop the bleeding till his pulse faded to nothing. At dawn, I helped lift his body into a bag, then zipped it up and tagged him.

The day before I'd gone out as a Forward Observer's RTO on a search and destroy mission, and returned with a new name, an identity that stayed with until I went home.

The F.O. said three words to me as we saddled up.

"Cantalupo?"

"Yeah."

"Stay close."

He was blondish, a Second Lieutenant, twenty-three maybe, a West-Pointer, straight and narrow as a lifer.

He'd been sent out on this "special operation" because Intel said an NVA Battalion was operating in the Ho Bo. Our company was the bait to have them engage. The F.O.'s job was to call in air and artillery support when they we got them in a firefight. Great plan except we'd be outnumbered six or eight to one until the support kicked in, which meant we were expendable. My job was to keep the F.O. alive and in communication with air and artillery support. I was his mouth and ears.

The company walked spread out in a clearing between two stands of trees. And as it often was on these missions, it was too quiet, like the moment when you stop breathing as your eye looks down the sight at a kill. Silent, and still, still like all the leaves, crickets, birds, and the whole natural world were ready for your rifle to erupt, the firefight to start, the ferocious battle to begin.

Then, in the midst of the stillness, from the right flank, one word:

"Incoming!!!"

Almost simultaneously, I heard mortars shooting out from tubes.

Poomff. Poomff. Poomff. Poomff.

Poomff. Poomff. Poomff. Poomff.

Before I could run for cover, an RPG exploded a few meters in front of me, ripping out chunks of elephant grass and someone's flesh.

I ate dirt pushing my face into the ground as flaming metal fragments tore by. Some soldier near me screamed, his elbow dangling muscle, ligaments, and veins like a frayed wall socket.

"Medic! MEDIC!!!"

Poomff. Poomff. Poomff. Poomff.

Another barrage walked toward us.

The F.O. split in one direction, I the other, and we kissed trees on opposite sides of the clearing. I pressed close against a thin rubber tree as splintered branches crashed down.

Another RPG exploded nearby. More screams. Moans.

Soldiers sprayed M-16 and M-60 rounds into the dense stands even though they knew whoever was firing at us was far out of range.

"RTO! RTO!!! Get over here!!!"

Fuck. I'd have to low-crawl between explosions to reach him. One hundred and twenty pounds of radio, ammunition, smoke, grenades, claymore mines, a poncho liner, an entrenching tool, and c rations were on my back and I'd have to cross fifteen to twenty meters of open ground to reach him. He carried about a third of that, but he was the officer and I was his RTO. It was my job to get the radio to him so he could call in support. Whatever else I felt was irrelevant.

I waited until the rounds walked off in another direction and low-crawled across the clearing like I had fire ants biting my ass.

About halfway across mortars starting walking up behind me. I scrambled across the remaining ten meters like a squirrel on speed. I dove into the strand of trees where he was hunkered down just as a mortar hit almost dead on the spot where I'd just crossed.

"You alright?"

"I'm here."

"Your radio's a mess," he shot as he ripped off the handset, put it to his mouth. "Let's hope this baby still works."

I swiveled round and felt the gashes in the PRC-25's metal body. The green canvas binding felt like the tattered edges of a flag.

That close. An inch or two lower and the shrapnel would have torn into my back, maybe my heart.

Aces, this time. Aces straight up all the way.

"Red Dragon One to Alpha Four, fire mission, do you read me?"

Static. Static, and then through the static and squelched silence an answer.

"This—is—Alpha—Four. Fire mission. Copy."

"Alpha four this is Red Dragon One, receiving mortar and RPG fire. You copy."

"Red Dragon One this is Alpha Four. What's your position?"

"We're at checkpoint Bravo Tango. You copy."

"We copy, Red Dragon. Bravo Tango. Hens out of coop."

Another mortar barrage smashed into the trees where we hugged the earth. Shattered branches fell on top of us, trees toppled over one atop the other as if an enormous chainsaw were cutting the trunks and limbs. The rounds seemed to be centered only on me and the lieutenant. Guys on the other side of the clearing looked over at us as if we were a bad omen. I looked around and realized we were the only ones on this side of the clearing, everyone else was hunkered down on the other side.

The lieutenant handed me his binoculars. I guess he thought if something happened to him I could take over.

"Ten o'clock. In the tree line."

Through the lens I could see mortar flashes about three thousand meters away like tiny mirrors glinting as they turned in the sun. The mortars were dug in and well-camouflaged, but my eyes were prime for such flashes and the binoculars brought them an arm's length away.

A red smoke plume billowed up nearby the flashes and the lieutenant barked into the mouthpiece.

"Red Dragon One to Alpha Four. Adjust right 100 meters. Fire for effect. I repeat. Fire for effect."

"Copy that, Red Dragon. Right 100 meters. Fire for effect."

Two more mortar rounds exploded in the tree branches above us, raining down branches, hot metal and leaves. Another three crashed into the clearing about fifteen meters away. Shrapnel tore off chunks of tree bark and hurled them toward us as we covered our heads, our cheeks pressed hard into the ground. A sharp twig cut my lip and I spit blood on the dark ground.

Close. So close. Five meters closer and we're dead.

The smoke and debris cleared and we could see the 155 millimeter rounds bursting in the brush and elephant grass where we saw the flashes.

Then silence. Nothing. The lieutenant panned the area with his binoculars, spotted three NVA soldiers running through the elephant grass to out left. He calculated their speed and called in.

"Red Dragon One to Alpha Four. Adjust Right 200. Fire for effect. I repeat. Adjust right 200. Fire for effect."

"Alpha Four to Red Dragon. Copy that. Adjust right 200. Fire for effect."

Boom! Boom! Boom! Boom!

Boom! Boom! Boom! Boom!

The artillery battery pumped out round after round.

A few seconds later, explosions bloomed from the elephant grass and hurled chunks of debris into the air. Hunks of earth and flesh flew up into the smoke and flame brushed sky like a swirling tornado, then rained down to nothing. The smoke and flames turned to embers and the sky returned to a grayer shade of blue.

One by one the soldiers on the other side of the clearing rose out of their hiding places and stumbled toward the lieutenant and I. Medics ran over to where a few moaning soldiers lay bleeding.

"Fuck me," laughed Devil. "Look at this shit."

I pulled the branches and debris off my body, sat up, and looked over to where he was standing with a few other soldiers. A ring of small mortar craters circled the place where the lieutenant and I were huddled.

A ragged semi-circle about twenty meters in diameter pock-marked the clearing. There were other craters, a few in the stand where the other soldiers took cover, but most of the damage was around us, the F.O. and I.

"That's some bad shit, " Lee added. "Baaa-addd!"

By this time, the lieutenant, bug-eyed as a preying mantis, tossed the branches and chunks of tree bark off him, brushed the dirt off of his fatigues, and stood up to see what everyone was looking at. He gazed at the craters constellated around where we hunkered down.

If you were up in a chopper, the spot where the lieutenant and I called in artillery would've looked like the center circle in a bulls-eye. The surrounding craters would've looked like the shot clusters in ever-widening rings with the closest ring represented by the last two mortars that exploded about ten meters from our position.

The lieutenant looked up from surveying the craters and starred hard into my eyes.

"You've got some serious bad luck working, troop!" he fumed, and walked away.

I don't know why he put it on me. Could've been him that owned the bad luck just as easily as I.

Still, seeing all the craters around us as if we were their only target worried me.

How'd they sight in on us, pinpointing where we were? Buddha and bad karma," I mused. "Fucking Buddha owned the Ho Bo.

Yeah, in the Ho Bo, god was on their side.

So why the hell did he tag me? I didn't have bad karma.

But the FO wasn't taking any chances. He kept his distance. On the other side of the clearing, he stopped and leaned up against a tree and lit a smoke. The flame danced in his palms, his hands shook, the cigarette quivered in his mouth.

He took a long drag, closed his eyes, and blew the smoke out leisurely as if that's all there was, the smoke swirling through his lungs and then out again, the smooth taste of the tobacco soothing his fear. After a while, his breathing slowed and the shakes stopped.

Fear, will do that, after.

He told me to keep ten meters between us and said he'd yell if he needed me, then he humped on ahead as we headed back to the perimeter, never saying another word to me.

The late afternoon sun beat down hard. I lay my radio and backpack down and lay back, dropping my flack jacket off my shoulders. The day's burden gone, I let the heat wash over me and daydreamed. I saw Janice, a beach in Monterey, her long legs entwined in mine--I might have dozed.

Around dusk, as Spike, Devil and I were heating up C's on heat tabs, six or eight shots—CRACK!-CRACK!-CRACK!—ripped across the perimeter before anyone could take cover or get a bead on where the sniper was.

I, along with everyone else who was near by, saw two orange tracers go directly through Spike's steel pot, come out the other side, and puncture the olive drab five gallon water can between Spike and I.

Spike, according to my eyes and the eyes of Devil, Mike, and Lee--as well as the other soldiers sitting around heating C's—should've owned a hole in his head and been dead or seriously wounded.

But he wasn't dead. He wasn't even shot. The rounds must have angled around his head and pierced the water cans which were slightly off the direct line between the sniper, Spike and myself. As Devil saw it, my presence must've influenced the direction of the rounds so that they went around Spike's head to get to the water cans at my feet. I must've possessed some kind of magnetic power over the bullets.

Not that Devil was the only one who fashioned a theory to fit the phenomenon they saw. Everyone looked at Spike, then the water cans, then me, and came up with an explanation for how the bullets could go through Spike's steel pot without going through his skull, and how they could end up puncturing the water cans between us.

"Mothafucker," Devil finally said as he picked up the water

can shooting water over our C's, "you've got some serious voodoo shit working, my man. Ser-i-ous!"

In the meantime, Lee shot four M-79 grenade rounds into the trees where he'd spotted one of the muzzle flashes. Boom! Boom! Boom! Boom!, exploded the rounds. Branches, crashed down, then a black-pajamaed body, falling out of the tree like a mannequin, landing in a crumpled heap on the ground.

Spike, who by this time came out of his stunned silence, gave me a shitty look.

"Keep the fuck away from me, Radio. You've got a magnet for shit."

Lee, Devil, Baby San, and I were standing in the mortar pit at Firebase Pershing, looking out across the horizon at the bursting flames from our 81 millimeter mortars.

We'd just finished H and I's—the four of us bull-shitting about home or cars or girls or something. Must've been about 10 at night.

None of us thought much of the H & I's.

One time a pagoda was targeted, another time a village suspected of being Viet Cong sympathizers, once a crossing along the Ho Chi Minh trail.

Sometimes, we loaded "white peter" rounds (white phosphorous)—"to do the most damage" we were told—though the damage we witnessed in Trang Bang among the villagers was horrific, wounds that the medics couldn't fix, that no one could heal, "willie peter" shrapnel that burned through arms and legs, and seethed through skulls and into brains.

We were standing there speaking in low voices, cupping Marlboros, laughing quietly.

No one heard a mortar fire, the poomf of an incoming round leaving the mortar tube. The round exploded while we were in mid-sentence, our laughter still rolling out of our lips. The explosion wasn't close, twenty meters away maybe. We dove down behind sandbags and waited, sure there were more to come.

But, nothing came. No flash out of the far darkness surrounding the perimeter. No mortar tubes poomf, poomf, poomfing another series of rounds. Just one lone mortar and no casualties. Just another explosion to fray our nerves a little as we x-ed out another day.

No casualties, except one, me.

I felt something punch me like a hard rubber mallet to my back as I dove for cover. When we were sure there was no more incoming, we got up. There was no target to fire back at so we decided it was safer to head back to our bunkers for the night.

I still felt a burning sensation between my shoulder blades so I took off my flak jacket.

"What's up, Radio?" Devil asked.

"Not sure. Felt something but I'm not sure what it was."

"Where?" He sprayed the red-lensed flashlight across my back.

"My right shoulder."

"Well, I'll be fucked. You got yourself another purple heart."

"What are you talking about?"

"Here, man," and he touched a hole in my shoulder blade where a trickle of blood dripped down.

"You need to go to the med station," said Lee.

"A million dollar wound if I ever saw one. A sure ticket home."

"Fuck you, Baby San. No one else got hit?"

"No, man. Just you. You're a real fucking magnet man, if

I've ever seen one." laughed Devil.

After that night, Spike and his buddies called me "Magnet Man", and stayed as far away from me as they could.

It was a cruel joke with ominous intent, but I took it seriously. I got careful, too careful, one-week-and-a-wake-up-short-timer careful.

Thoughts of death and dying invaded my wakeful dreams. I realized I could die, could be dead already if it weren't for a two-inch high sandbag, or a bullet someone else took in my place.

My first five months I'd rarely thought about dying. Now I thought about it a hundred times a day.

No, I was no longer immortal.

My time was coming.

All the mortars and the RPGs and the AK bullets were written with my name.

So far I was lucky, but the day was coming, maybe this day, or maybe tomorrow.

Maybe tomorrow I'd trip a booby trapped-wire, or my radio's antenna would catch a sniper's squinting eye.

Maybe tomorrow, my time would come.

My lips brush the blond hairs along Janice's upper thighs. Her breath catches in a slight moan.

"Oh. Ohhh. Oh, god."

The earth shakes viciously and I wake with a blue-balled hard-on, the bunker shivering like a cowed dog.

Explosions burst all around me and dirt hails down on the sandbag roof. Red-hot shrapnel fragments tear through the green, sandbagged mortar pits and smash into the fleshy water cans and wooden ammo boxes.

I flick on my red-lensed flashlight, pull my jungle boot laces tight, and stumble toward the doorway.

Screams rise out of the explosions, then moans, then curses, shouts. I run up the bunker's first two steps, stick my head out the doorway.

Flashes rose out of the pitch-black sky with deafening explosions. Close. Closer. Fires igniting all around.

Soldiers silhouetted by the flames leap into foxholes and mortar pits and vanish. Three silhouettes run out of the bunker to my right and into the mortar pit about thirty feet from my bunker. Two others run into a second pit.

I stand there, one leg in and one leg out of the doorway. Suddenly, I am hit with the shakes.

I'm halfway in and halfway out of the doorway. We are under an intense mortar and rocket attack--screams, explosions, bodies running for cover. A blur of shadows moving inside the pits.

I stand there frozen, unable to move, unable to step out of the bunker for the terror in my body.

I stand there paralyzed, shaking, riddled with guilt, watching my buddies running through explosions to reach the mortar pit and fire back.

No, I am no longer immortal.

I am afraid, my body frozen, unable to obey commands.

I stand there as Mike, Baby San, and Lee frantically throw mortars into the tubes to fire back while rockets and mortars explode in the smoke and chaos around them.

I stand there on the edge of the steps, half in and half out of the doorway, brushed in shadow and light, unable to charge out into the explosions, to run through the smoke and flames to help them fire back. I am numb, shaking from too many close calls, too many death rattles rattling in my brain.

In dim, effervescent light, eerie as ghosts stirring in a graveyard, I watch Mike, Baby San, and Lee guiding mortar rounds into the tube and firing out into the night.

I know I should be there with them breaking down rounds, sliding mortars into the tubes.

I know I should be there despite the terror, despite the mortars raining down around us, despite my fear.

But I am shot, "shell shocked", my nerves frayed as live wires, my legs short-circuited by terror.

Five months earlier, I broke down rounds as blood poured down my face. Now, I can't even move to step out of the doorway, nor stop my body from quaking in terror.

Explosions crash into bunkers around Mike and the others. I hear screams, moans, curses.

In the other pit, Devil and Spike finally start sliding rounds into the tube. Flashes burst up from the tube and frame them in red and orange flames.

"Radio! Radio! Where the fuck is Radio?"

I hear Spike's voice calling me, but I still can't move.

A rocket explodes next to the pit where Mike, Baby San, and Lee are pouring out rounds. The explosion blows a gaping hole in the pit, knocks all three of them down.

I hear Mike cursing.

"Motherfuckers!! Hand me a round!"

Lee hands him a round, but doesn't stand up. I can only see his arm and the mortar, and Mike grabbing it and slipping it into the tube in a croutch. I can't see Baby San anymore.

"Come on! Come on! Hand me some more rounds!" Mike is screaming, but only Lee is handing him rounds. "Baby San!?"

"He's hit, Mike!" Lee screams.

"Keep handing me rounds! Don't fucking stop! Medic!!! Medic!!!"

From the other pit, I hear Spike's voice calling.

"Radio! Radio!"

I force my legs to move, run four or five steps and fall down, scrunch up against the wall of Mike's bunker, shaking.

"Fuck! Fuuuck!!!' I can't stop shaking and I can't get my legs to move. I start low-crawling toward Devil and Spike.

"Lee!!! Hand me some fucking rounds, goddamnit! How's Baby San?"

"He's fucked up!"

"Medic! Medic!!!"

I'm about ten feet from the mortar pit's opening when another rocket explodes.

I'm blown backwards and smash into a wall of sandbags.

I hear Mike screaming, but it's muted now, distant, like a voice coming out of a tunnel, a muffled echo.

"Medic!!! Medic!!! Lee!!! Lee!!? Hand me some fucking rounds!"

Explosions burst all around us, but I can barely hear them, and I'm fading away, drifting into blackness.

A medic kneels over me, waking me up.

I have an enormous headache, but I'm not wounded. I hear Mike's voice.

"Medic!!! Medic!!!"

"Relax, Mike. We're here. We're doing everything we can."

Someone's in a body bag near where Mike is sitting.

I try to sit up.

"Whoa! Whoa! Hold on, Radio. Lay back down. Just rest, man. You're alright."

"Where's Baby San? I told him to get down."

"He's gone, Mike. He's gone!"

"He can't be fucking gone. He was just here. He was just fucking here!"

Mike bounds over to the body bag and starts unzipping it. He pulls it open and I see Baby San's bloody face.

"Stop, man. Stop!"

Two medics pull Mike off the body bag. Take him back to where he was, sit him down. One lights a cigarette and hands it to him.

"He's gone, Mike. You gotta let him go."

Mike draws from the cigarette, lets the smoke cloud his face. He stares at me, but doesn't see me, I don't exist anymore.

Two more body bags are laid beside Baby San.

"You find his arm?"

"A piece. A hand and..."

"What about the black guy?"

"Yeah, he's mostly there."

"You see that rocket crater?"

"Musta been a 122. Pit looks like a moon crater."

"Why the fuck were they outside the bunkers?"

"Mortar guys. That's their job. They run outside to fire back when everyone's running for cover."

"Crazy, man. I couldn't fucking do it."

"Yeah, like firemen running into a fire."

"Without a hose or a ladder to get out."

"War's war. Ain't no planning for the future, 'less you're dead, or dying."

"What about that famous million-dollar wound?"

"In the 'Nam? How long you been here? Aweek? Ain't no million dollar wound here, man. If you ain't dead enough, limbless, or blind, you ain't going home."

"I ain't even supposed to be here. I'm a conscientious-objector. Jehovah's Witness."

"Well, now you're witnessing as a medic. Only good part is six months and we're done."

"FTA, man. FTA, all the way."

"Only bad part is we don't usually last six months. Let's get these guys down to the LZ, I'm tired of looking at them."

"You wanna medevac the RTO?"

"No, he'll be alright. They'd send him back soon as they see he ain't bleeding anyway."

"Aces and Eights, man. Aces and Eights all the way down the line."

I watched them take Devil, Baby San, and Spike down to the LZ, heard the medevac chopper them out of my life.

Whomp. Whomp. Whomp.

And then silence.

Where Shadows End

Three days passed while I moved in and out of limbo—conscious, unconscious, numb, not feeling my body, the bandages peeled off my open wounds.

Three days of waking and drifting back into my brain trauma induced coma, drifting somewhere between the living and the dead.

And when I awoke,I didn't know where I was.

I remembered the mortar exploding a few feet away, my body hurled up into the dark sky and then crashing down.

I remembered the warm blood drenching my back, arms picking me up, my body bouncing up and down as I was carried into the bunker.

I tried to sit up but my legs and arms were too heavy to lift. I lay back, closed my eyes, and slipped into a dreamless sleep.

When I opened my eyes again, a nurse was sitting beside me.

"Good morning. How do you feel?"

"Tired. Very, very tired. How long did I sleep?"

"Three days."

"I don't remember much."

"You remember Dr. Chang?"

"The brain doctor?"

"Neurosurgeon."

"Yes."

"How are you feeling?"

"I…I don't know. I can't feel much."

"Do you have pain?"

"No. A little."

"Where?"

"All over, I guess."

"No sharp pain anywhere? Your chest? Your head?"

"Uh…yes. Some. My head. My arm."

"Are you nauseous?"

"No...no."

"Are you hungry?"

"No…not really. I can't really feel…I can't…I feel…I feel like my body's not…there."

"You need to eat. I'll let the doctor know you're awake."

When the nurse returned with Doctor Chang, I was asleep. I felt a hand gently touch my shoulder and opened my eyes to find the doctor leaning over me checking the incision on my skull.

"Good morning. How are you feeling?"

"I…uh. I just feel kind of numb."

"That's the pain medication, the Demerol. So, no head pain? No sharp ache anywhere?"

"No."

"How's your arm?"

"I can't really feel it?"

"Can you squeeze my hand?"

I think left arm. I think squeeze.

"More. A little more."

I think hard, squeeze hard.

"Okay. That's fine. I'm going to keep you on the Demerol for a few more days."

"Doctor…am I--?"

"You're fine. You're going to be fine. You just need to rest, try to eat."

"I can't...feel-- "

"Your body's going to be numb for awhile. We're going to decrease your pain medication, but you need to tell the nurse if you feel any sharp pains in your head or chest. You understand?"

"Yes."

"If you wake up with any sharp pain or any nausea you need to call the nurse immediately, you understand?"

"Yes."

"Now the nurse is bringing you some soup. You need to try to eat some, okay?"

"Okay."

"I'll be back this afternoon to look at you. Doctor Wilhelm is going to check your other injuries. If you're feeling any unusual pain in your arm, chest, or neck, you need to let him know. Now eat some soup."

"I just--."

"Nurse, make sure he eats. Soup. Jello. Even if it's just a few bites."

"Yes, doctor. Do you want me to wake him up to eat?"

"Not today. Tonight, yes. But you can let him sleep after you feed him this morning."

"Doctor, I--"

"Don't worry. You're fine. You're doing fine."

When you return from limbo you do not enter through a door.

Or maybe the door revolves: One moment you are shadow, the next, you are alive.

There is no day, nor night.

After I awoke from brain surgery—sometimes in pain, sometimes with a dull ache radiating out of every pore in my body—a nurse would come and redress my bandages.

Three times a day. Every day.

And every day I would wait anxiously for my ritual of unbearable pain.

PAIN with block letters.

BURNING, PIERCING, THROBBING PAIN.

PULSATING PAIN LIKE A NEON SIGN PULSATING OUT OF HELL.

If this were torture, I would've answered anything I was asked. I would have lied, begged, confessed, offered up a finger, a hand, one shrunken nut to stop the nurse from ripping off the bloody bandages stuck to the ragged nerves and raw flesh of my wounds.

But this torture wasn't meant to stop, and no one wanted to ask questions.

I guess my body answered for me, my answers written in the deep gouges of my wounds.

Yellowish plasma and dried blood saturated the gauze bandages.

If infection set in, the plasma turned green or yellow-green like baby shit.

If the baby shit colored fluid oozed out of the open wound, the doctor would have to gouge out more flesh till they extracted the infected part, or they might have to sever the whole arm or leg if the infection was too large.

What would happen if the wound in my neck got infected?

How could a surgeon dig out the infection from my juggler vein?

Only way to stop an infection in my neck wound was to sever my head.

Only way to cure an infection in my head was to extract my brain.

Only way to kill the infection in my mind was to sever me from myself.

So, for the first few days, with all the pain medication dripping through the I.V., the sharp tearing of the gauze, the peeling of dried bandages away from the ragged wound, I was numb, the fiery burning that increased as the pain medication diminished.

And the revolving door between limbo and life turned in that music of pain.

I caught my scream in my throat, bit my tongue as the gauze slowly peeled a new layer of scab away.

I swallowed, grunted, grit my teeth, felt streams of salt-water slide down my cheeks. And as the drugs wore off and the dosage of painkillers decreased, I learned to endure higher and higher levels of the excruciating, screaming pain, and the door back to limbo slowly stopped turning.

Soon, only pain defined my waking existence.

Not the head pain the neurosurgeon worried over, but the pain of raw flesh being torn off each wound three times a day.

The nurse would come with her cart of gauze and tape and pills. She would check my I.V. drip, look at the waves and numbers flickering and undulating on the screens above my head, ask how I was feeling, then take out her scissors and slide the blade under the tape on my left shin and cut a line from one end of the bandage to the other.

Her fingers worked quickly then, peeling a flap away from the raw wound so she could firmly grip the tape. Then she would rip away the new skin in one rapid tear.

Thirteen rips, three times a day, day after day.

Thirteen cuts.

Thirteen peels.

Thirteen tears.

Then a lapse, a moment between synaptic impulse and connection, a space between the act and the effect, before a fireball of pain would shoot through my nerves and bright crimson blood would rise from the pink gash.

No, you do not return from limbo through an open door.

You turn and turn and turn until the certainty of the physical realm returns, till the pain or desire or despair brings you back and the hazy world of non-being dies, consumed by the internal combustion of your body.

I awoke from limbo day by day, the pain medication slowly decreasing; the pain in my open wounds diminishing till there was no more than the sharp tears and my own swallowed scream.

I went from broth and jello to oatmeal and beef stew, my body a bombed-out pagoda, my future a crater from a five-hundred pound bomb.

And when I came out of that dazed, uncharted territory on the borders between the living and the dead, I did not arrive in the world I left behind.

I arrived in another place, a place as uncharted as the region in my brain where the shrapnel lay, where the neurosurgeon extracted them from the gray matter of my life.

When I was stable enough to travel, I left Bien Hoa. The medics strapped me onto a gurney and rolled me up through the mouth of the C-130 and into the belly where a whole line of bodies were locked and loaded down.

We must have looked like living body bags with our olive drab blankets wrapped tightly around us, our I.V.s swaying from the poles above.

I can't remember the flight or the landing.

Maybe I was asleep.

Maybe there was nothing to remember, just the uneventful journey from one hospital to another, from the place where you go to die or survive, to the place where you wait to go home.

What I do remember is Saigon, the hospital there, and Peaches, the nurse who I came to love.

Peaches wasn't her real name, but that's what everyone called her, Peaches was who she was in Vietnam.

Peaches after Peaches and Cream maybe, a sugar-coated dessert to touch the spot in your belly where something more was wanted, where you craved what was missing from the meals, the meds, and the healing.

Peaches like a Georgia Peach, except Peaches didn't come from Georgia. She didn't have peachy cream cheeks like a Norman Rockwell portrait.

Her dark, pageboy styled hair was wild with sweat and the dusty air and didn't frame her face like a snapshot from home.

No, she was more common than beautiful, more flawed human than air-brushed bunny.

But, when I say I loved her, I did.

She, more than anyone else, kept me alive during the month I lay in a hospital in Saigon.

Her smile, open as an unwritten page, woke me from my morning dreams and drifted with me as I slipped into my evening sleep.

"You want a bullet?"

"You got one?" I quipped.

She'd take an imaginary bullet from her pocket and place it in my mouth.

"How's that taste?"

"Sweet as a Georgia peach."

"Bite down now." and she tore the first bandage off my leg.

When the burning screamed from shin to brain, I bit down so hard on her imaginary bullet I split my tongue.

"Sweet," I smiled, tears welling in my eyes.

"Vampire," and then she peeled another bandage off.

The pain was excruciating, but her imaginary bullet helped, and after a few days I stopped biting into my tongue and breathed through the pain.

Somehow, Peaches ripping off my gauze bandages was less painful. There was a caring, an intimacy, a dance as if between two lovers, that helped me swallow the pain.

Peaches was from Indiana, a mid-western girl, twenty-two maybe, a year out of nursing school. She'd volunteered, wanted to help, serve her country--that's what she told me.

Now, six months into her year in Saigon, she was tired.

"I'm just…you know…too many…I've seen too many boys…" and then she trailed off, the words slipping out of her mouth before she could catch them.

Too many boys, too many fucked up boys, wasted by a fucked up war, and I was one of them, fucked up, lost somewhere between what I was and what I'd become.

Too many lives forever changed.

Too many fake smiles to cover grief.

Too many questions she could only answer with lies.

Days slid past my hospital window, slid out over the Saigon horizon like an orange flare parachuting down from the blue, smoke-streaked sky.

Days and then weeks, the light through the bamboo blinds casting bars of shadow as I lay.

West.

My window faced west, the western sky, the place where the horizon ended and darkness dragged a train of stars and a moon when it passed.

I asked Peaches to keep my blinds open so that I could see the sparks and streams of firefights punctuated by the far-off rat-tat-tat of AK's and M-16s.

Peaches said the firefights were too far away to hear, that all we could hear from the hospital were the rumble of B-52s dropping bombs, an artillery battery from the edge of the city, that I was seeing firefights in my mind.

"No, I can hear them. Small patrols ambushed in the jungle, a platoon in deep shit, I hear everything."

"That's your imagination talking. You still wish you were there."

"With my platoon? No. I was done with the war before the war was done with me. No, what I hear is real. Ghosts. Live ghosts."

"You're a live ghost," she mocked.

"Yeah, I guess I am."

I stare up at the white ceiling sky of my cubicle in Saigon and wonder why my wounds still cry out to me—loss, loss, the ache of the dead, of dead buddies and dead Vietnamese, of the hating eyes of mama and papa sans starring out from inside my chest, my heart pierced with tiny metal fragments that will never heal.

I wonder how the x-rays show a constellation of mortar fragments around and through my heart, a constellation that reminds me of a star, a star made of metal, of bronze, every time I see x-rays of my heart.

Maybe Peaches was right.

As I lay in my bed, reality was as fragmentary as my terror dreams.

Past and present, inside and outside, the war I remembered and the war that droned on and on, coalesced into images I could not decipher as real or unreal.

Demerol, she said,--the drug I was taking for brain pain--demerol created hallucinations, sleeping and waking dreams where one scene sifted into another like jump-cuts without continuity or contextual connections.

In a Demerol world, there was no interior and exterior reality. There was merely the emotional context of the hallucination, of the scene played out in my brain.

But after awhile my world and the Demerol world seemed the same.

Days slid into nights and nights drifted into bad dreams. Images drenched with fear, grief, love, hate, jump-cut from one to another. All was real, all, a dream.

The only certainty I knew was the bed where I lay, the sounds of nurses and doctors and wounded soldiers passing by, the hushed voices, moans, and wheels rolling past.

And Peaches, waking me in the morning with my breakfast and my meds. Peaches smiling, asking me how I felt that morning, if I was ready to have my bandages changed, her soft, warm fingers against my lips as she placed an imaginary bullet in my mouth, as she slid the scissors under the tape and cut.

I was fucked up, but I would survive. I would get better. I would return home.

But what did going home mean?

Would I be able to move my left arm or would it just remain limp at my side as now?

What did my face look like under the gauze?

I didn't ask for a mirror. I didn't want the revelation. Not then. Not any time soon.

I looked at the deep, angry gouges of the open wounds on my chest, legs, and arm each time Peaches peeled the gauze off, and I hated what I saw.

This wasn't me. This wasn't the I I remembered.

I was an athlete. I loved to play football, baseball, to box, to swim. I was a wrestler in college before I got drafted.

And now…

I would get better, but no, I wouldn't wrestle again, not with a limp left arm, not with a broken skull filled in with bone cartilage.

I'd awakened from brain surgery new, with a new unlived life, but I didn't know who I was. My wife, my mother, my friends were waiting for my return, but something more than shrapnel had been removed from my brain.

The I that made me I had been extracted along with the shrapnel in my brain. I woke from the surgery blank, the only emotional connection to the past began shortly before and after the explosion. There were no faces in my dreams, not faces from home anyway, not faces I recognized as my own.

As I lay in the unlit room staring up at the blank ceiling sky, I could not imagine a single face, not Janice's, not my mother's, no one's.

If a face emerged from the darkness, it was dead: Lonny's face, Devil's, Baby San's.

Vietnamese faces. Faces from the village of Trang Bang. Faces with gone eyes and dead stares. Faces without mouths. Faces on heads without bodies. Faces floating down a black river without a name.

Beyond my window in Bien Hoa, beyond the hospital in Saigon, the war went on.

In the dark, the flickering shadows cast by flares parachuting down, the whomp, whomp, whomp of mortars and artillery, the staccato arguments between AKs and M16s, the droning rumble of the B-52s carpet-bombing the Earth, went on and on.

But I could not see my face, my body's silhouette patrolling among the images I saw in my night terrors. There were only shadows in the flat, grey plaster ceiling, only the phantasmagoria of war.

A war that was no longer mine.

I was a shadow among shadows, a silhouette flat as a pop-up target on the rifle range at Fort Ord.

I was the shadow where light ended, the shadow in the light.

"You'll be heading home soon," Peaches said one afternoon. "The doctor put you on the list."

I was completely in love with her by then. As she leaned over my chest to readjust my I.V. tube, I felt her warm breasts against me and got an immediate hard on. And as I gazed up at her eyes I saw desire there, just a glimpse, desire mixed with sadness, desire mixed with unrequited love.

"I love you." I blurted.

"I love you too," she smiled. "Now eat. Show me your love by eating everything on your tray."

"No, I mean it. I love you."

She just looked at me.

I know she saw my hardness, my desire. I could see the dark, pink areole of her hardened nipple through the olive green scrubs, her dark, brown hair fall across her eyes hiding her own strange desire, her light pink lips moist as the pulp of a plum.

I was so in love with her, the pain of her body rubbing against my open wounds felt like a gesture of love.

I couldn't make love to her, even if I wanted, even if she desired me the way I wanted her. My wounded body wouldn't have allowed it.

But, after six months of starving for love in the bush, I could devour her with my eyes. And in my Demerol dreams, I could taste her peach-pink nipples despite my wounds. And I could hear her cry out in ecstasy as I kissed every peak and valley and crevice of her body.

I was getting better, healing a month after my near death. My hard on was a sign.

Peaches knew every inch of my body and knew my physical being better than my wife, or mother. She'd washed and cleaned and dressed every muscle and gash. She'd seen every orifice, touched every place I called my own. She'd touched the throbbing heat of my groin, my legs, my feet, my arms. She'd weighed the weight of my heart, the number of beats per minute that kept me alive, that rose and fell with the proximity of her body heat next to mine. She'd felt my warm palm, the hot sparks she inspired simply by washing my hands. She'd watched the gold flecks in my hazel eyes flicker when she came to my bed and watched as I took in every subtle gesture of her care.

Yes, she knew me better than anyone. She's seen me wake from the limbo of passing on to the wakefulness of agonizing pain. She'd seen me wake with fear and apprehension that I was no longer who I was, that there was something missing, some synaptic gap too far to cross, something gone from the old I and this new unknown I with scars and broken connections.

She'd come in many times as I stared at the ceiling asking the same questions over and over in my mind.

Who am I if I am not who I was, if I cannot remember or connect emotionally with my past, with the person who I used to be?

And so when she told me I would be going to Japan soon, transferred to the Air Force Hospital in Yokohama as soon as the neurosurgeon cleared me for the long flight, I was sad, struck by a grief two parting lovers' might feel.

"So you're kicking me out huh?"

"Don't you want to go home?"

"I don't know. I'm not...you know."

"Your wife's there, your family."

"I don't...I can't...remember...them."

"You can't remember your family?"

"I can't really picture their faces. The only people I can imagine are dead."

"What about the guys who put you on the med evac, the guys who saved you?"

"Mike, Lee, yeah, I can still see them, but mostly I see silhouettes, vague shadows."

"But what about when you're awake? What about now?"

"I can't see any faces, no."

"You can't picture your wife?"

"I picture her, but there's nothing there."

"What do you mean nothing?"

"No emotions. No love. I can't even feel myself in the picture."

"Have you told the doctor about this?"

"What's to tell?"

"That you have no emotional connection with your family, that something got cut in your brain."

"I don't even know if that's true. Maybe I just can't remember."

"Maybe you just need time to heal."

"Maybe I'm a duck. Quack. Quack."

"Maybe I'm a chicken."

"Cock-a-doodle-doo!"

"Your crazy."

"Now that I can tell the doctor."

"You need to talk to him before you leave."

"About?"

"About this. He should know how you're feeling."

"You want me to tell him about us?"

"You know what I mean."

"I'm in lust for you that's my emotional connection."

"You are a duck!"

"Don't you love me a little?"

Her eyes betrayed her. She moved away from the bed to create some distance between us.

But it wasn't enough, it would never be enough. Her face was imprinted on my brain, and I'm sure mine would come back to her many years later, long after she'd forgotten Vietnam. Something happened between us, some emotional bond that we would both carry forward through the years.

I loved her, I really did. She, more than anyone, saved my life.

Maybe it was her imaginary bullet.

Maybe it was the way her hands touched each open wound with a kind of compassion I'd never known.

Maybe it was how we each needed the touch of the other to survive the devastation we found around us.

Maybe, in another place and another time, we would have fallen in love, or been lovers, or found our way together through this unforgiving world.

But in Vietnam, we just moved on like shadows passing through the dusk, touching each other for a flash, a twilight instant, and then slipping away, disappearing into night's long shadow.

Peaches gave me one last look as she strapped me to the gurney and the medics rolled me away, down the ramp and out onto the tarmac to be loaded onto the belly of the plane, her palm squeezing mine as Lonny's once had, squeezing, then slowly letting her hand slide out of mine, kissing my forehead and waving good bye.

"See ya, ducky."

"Yeah, see ya back in The World."

The flight to Japan is gone from me now.

Or maybe I was never there.

Maybe I was in my Demerol dream, humping down a kaleidoscopic trail, black mambos and Bengali tigers poking their heads through the multi-colored fronds.

I don't remember crossing the sea, nor floating through clouds, nor the rock and roll of the C-130 as it rode on the currents to Japan.

I remember Devil calling, Lonny squeezing my hand and letting go. I remember bodies buffeted against me, and slipping away on a dark river I could not name.

But I cannot tell you what it felt like to rise out of the heat and stench of Vietnam, to leave behind the putrefied misery of war and fly over the sea, or what the airbase and hospital looked like when we landed.

Out of the Demerol dream of snakes, tigers, and palm fronds, I woke to a stranger's moans, to the stark, white walls of the Yokohama hospital and a small, round-faced Japanese nurse gazing down at me as if I were some exotic, dangerous animal.

I do not remember the flight, the crossing, or the arrival.

All that remained, was Peaches' kiss, the lingering warmth of her palm, Baby San's voice, Lonny's whisper, Devil's smile, the tender squeeze of a hand holding onto a world, and then letting go.

Other books by rg cantalupo

The Light Where Shadows End
an autobiographical novel

Thank You For Your Service
an autobiographical novel

The Endurance:

Journey Toward Worlds End
a lyrical novel

Private Entries
a poetic diary of war

No Thanks
war poems and stories

Walking Water On Earth
poems and stories

The Art of Naming
poems and stories

rgcantalupo.com

From *Kill Today, So Tomorrow Will Not Come*

"I'm done with half-truths.
I'm done with being told I'm going to get better when I don't know who I am, or who I was.
I need to see my face.
I need to see the Ihidden under the gauze bandage that's covered my head for the past two months."

CPSIA information can be obtained
at www.ICGtesting.com
Printed in the USA
LVHW091402200221
679500LV00029B/664